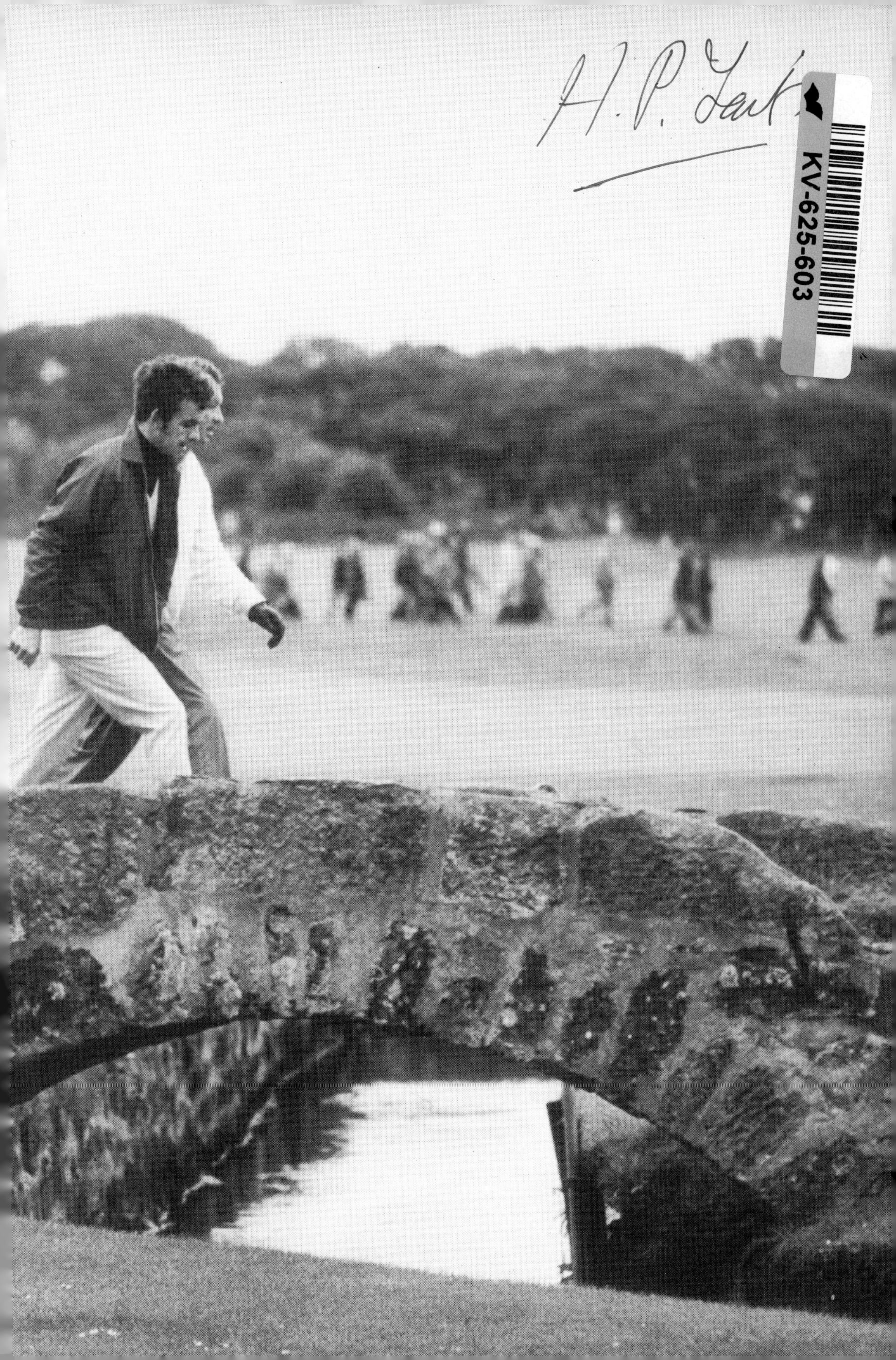

TONY JACKLIN
The Price of Success

TONY JACKLIN
The Price of Success

Liz Kahn

Hamlyn
London · New York · Sydney · Toronto

To David and Richard,
    Vivien, Bradley,
    Warren, Tina and
    Chris

Front endpaper: Crossing the bridge with Alex Caygill at the 18th
at St Andrews in the 1970 Open
Title page: Putting on the last green when winning the Dunlop Masters
at Sandwich, 1967

Published by The Hamlyn Publishing Group Limited
London · New York · Sydney · Toronto
Astronaut House, Feltham, Middlesex, England

ISBN 0 600 35272 2

Filmset in England by Tradespools Ltd, Frome, Somerset
Printed and bound in Great Britain by
Hazell Watson & Viney Ltd, Aylesbury, Bucks

Contents

Introduction

MENTION THE NAME Tony Jacklin and there's an astonishing reaction. It may be one of aggression or hurt pride from a disappointed golfing public who idolised his success. Equally, there are staunch admirers who retain their elation at his past achievements and their faith in his future ones. But always the same question lingers on. Just what did happen to Tony Jacklin? Certainly everyone is prepared to hold forth in explaining what happened to Tony and why it happened – trying to simplify a highly complex question which intrigues them. The opinions vary from he just wasn't good enough to he was a quitter, he became rich too quickly, he lost his ambition, he had it too easy, he took drugs, he came out of America too soon, he was too cocky, he didn't practise enough, he got the twitch, it was the fault of the Press. All these theories and many more are put forward to explain Tony Jacklin's decline from being a national hero whom everyone was proud to claim to becoming a golfer who was struggling with his game, who was thinking about making the cut and sometimes missing it. It should be pointed out though that he was always mercurial – before he won the 1969 Open Championship he missed the cut in America three times in a row.

The saga of Tony Jacklin is an interesting story. But it *is* a story and not just a few words of explanation that can be tossed off in a couple of sentences to explain the very heart and soul of a man who did what no other British golfer has ever done.

Since Tony won the Open Championship at Royal Lytham and St Annes and then went on to win the United States Open Championship, there has appeared little prospect of any young British golfer emulating his remarkable achievements. He won those two major championships within the space of a year. He won two Jacksonville Open titles on the tough American Tour. He finished fifth in the 1970 Open Championship at St Andrews where, in the opening round, he covered the first nine holes in an astonishing 29 strokes only to have the momentum interrupted by thunder and lightning which postponed the finish of the round until the next day. He finished third in the 1971 Open Championship at Royal Birkdale, two strokes behind the winner, Lee Trevino, and again, in 1972 in the Open Championship at Muirfield, he finished third, two strokes behind Trevino. During this time he was also winning other tournaments in Britain and in other parts of the world but his loss to Trevino in that 1972 Open Championship, when the American cruelly chipped in on the 71st hole, was probably the most significant point of his career.

It takes motivation, energy, ambition, aggression and talent to achieve anything at the highest level and Tony certainly put everything he had into reaching the top. Maybe we underestimate the enormity of his achievement and the toll it took.

In this book, Tony has been incredibly honest about himself and much of the text is a verbatim account of his attitudes. He recognises that he is a person apart—he retains the mantle of success, that indefinable aura which makes people back off at the same time as they press forward wanting to claim him. He is frank about his golf, his selfishness, his emotions, his relationships and his future. In order to create a balance, his family, friends, fellow professionals, manager and the Press have contributed by talking about Tony Jacklin as they know and see him.

It's not easy to be a hero and Tony had the guts to put himself up to be shot down. Possibly he resents some of the impositions his success has created but, inevitably, they are the price heroes must be prepared to pay.

Maybe this book will give a greater perspective of the man who is Tony Jacklin.

Liz Kahn

1: Early Days

ON 7TH JULY, 1944, Anthony Jacklin, son of Doris and Arthur, was born at Scunthorpe General Hospital, Lincolnshire, weighing a lusty 10 lb. By the time he was nine months old he was walking. 'He was never still,' says Arthur, 'and it caused him to rupture his stomach. He had to go into hospital to have it seen to, and it was the most worrying time of my life. I had it firmly fixed in my mind that he wouldn't come out of the anaesthetic – he seemed too small. When we were told that he'd had the operation and he was all right, it was as though they'd lifted the world off me. He came out of hospital and then three weeks later he ruptured the other side, and went back in to have that done. He's never had any trouble with it since.

'I know you always think the world of your own, but Tony was a bit special as a kid. I remember him digging the garden with a huge spade when he was only four, and he jumped on it to get it to go down. He was always very active.'

Doris and Arthur Jacklin still live in Scunthorpe in a modest bungalow. They are warm-hearted, welcoming people, who have both worked hard all their lives. 'We're an emotional family, we're feeling people,' says Arthur, and because of their emotions and their individuality, the Jacklin household was sometimes a tempestuous one. Both Doris and Arthur have a strong streak in them, and Tony inherited it.

Their daughter, Lynn, was born 22 months after Tony. 'He was never jealous of her in any way,' says Doris, 'he was marvellous. They were both easy children to bring up.'

Arthur worked as an engine driver at the main industry of the town, the Scunthorpe steelworks, where he graduated from steam to electric engines, and finally to driving a lorry. Doris worked in the dress business, and she made all the children's clothes.

Doris was also a fine soprano singer and was greatly involved in the Scunthorpe Amateur Operatic Society, where she took leading roles in such productions as *Glamorous Night*, *Bitter Sweet*, *Desert Song* and *Vagabond King*. 'I would play whatever role it was at home,' recalls Doris. 'If you have a part on stage, you never come out of it, until the last curtain call is over. That is me, and that's how I was. If I was going out singing, no one could talk to me before I went, I wanted to be left alone to do my own thing. I think it was understood at home and they were keen enough to help me with my roles.

'Tony came on stage and brought on the bouquets in *Glamorous Night* when he was about 14. He sang nicely and used to like singing. He had a nice voice.

'I would like to have sung professionally. I would have been very ambitious were it not for the family and the lack of money to get someone to look after them. As it was, I felt if you have children–you give up going on the stage.

'I've never voiced it before in the family, but I can say now that it was hard for me seeing Tony going forwards, though there wasn't anything I wouldn't have done for him. It was only a few years ago, that we were out for dinner with Tony in London, and he said to me that I ought to have kept on singing and got to the top, because that had really been my biggest disappointment. And, more than I've ever said, it was frustrating because the potential was there.'

Tony and his mother have had a difficult relationship at times because in many ways they are very alike. 'It was easy for Tony and me to clash– you won't get a stronger personality than his,' says Doris. From his mother, Tony inherited the ambitious, independent streak, the theatrical ability to switch on and off, the mimicry, and some of the emotional content. 'I'm terribly emotional and have very strong feelings,' says Doris. 'I'd rather be like that than be hard, but I wish I didn't get quite so involved through my feelings.'

Tony admired and resented his mother, certainly his personality clash with her encouraged him to go out and show what he could do. 'First and foremost, my mother is a very talented woman, she was a marvellous singer. Then she got married, had kids, and really I think she found that hard. When I became successful, she saw what she could have been. She is very single-minded, which is terrific, but it is difficult in a family situation. She has the type of personality, where if she were on her own, doing what she wanted, it would all work for her. Obviously my Mum and I are so alike, it's unbelievable. Fortunately, I have, through my golf, been able to get out my individuality. My mother ended up frustrated because she had nowhere to channel her drive, motivation and talent.'

Even if she was not, according to Tony, the perfect mother, Doris had fire and spirit: 'Sometimes at weekends, when the kids were little, I would go out singing for 30 shillings a night, when we were short of money.'

When Tony was nine he took up golf, playing with his father who had recently taken up the game. 'In four years,' says Arthur, 'I got down to six handicap, and by the time Tony was 14 he was beating me two out of three times. I could see his potential, he lived, dreamed, ate and slept golf. There was no one close to him in Lincolnshire.

'He won the Lincolnshire Boys' Championship, which was open to 18-year-olds, at 13, 14, and then when he was 15 it came to the local course at Ashby. Tony shot 80 in the morning and he came in with a bit of an upset smile on his face. I told him there was nothing to smile about and he should get stuck into it in the afternoon. He went out in 33, back in 33, broke the professional course record with his five under par round, and won the championship by at least 15 strokes. It was unbelievable.

'The two of us used to argue a lot on the golf course, and although he was often right, I would get on to him about things. He would moan and groan if a shot wasn't quite right because he was always looking for perfection. I didn't like his moaning and said so. But I was very proud of him and we had a close relationship.

'He hit thousands of golf shots every week. He would be practising in a bunker when people went out to play their round, and still be in the same bunker when they got back. He was really dedicated.

'When Tony was 16, both he and I entered the Lincolnshire Open, which was for professionals and amateurs, and was being played at nearby Elsham. In the morning Tony shot 74 and was tied with a scratch player for the lead; I shot 77 and was tied second. After lunch there was a tremendous gale-force wind – you could lie on it – and I thought I was doing pretty well to go out in 40. Tony was out in 35 and finished with a 71. He won the championship, beating the professionals by nine shots and the amateurs by 12 shots – it was a tremendous performance.

'I remember when Tony was about 16, he said he would like to play in the British Boys' Championship at Dalmahoy in Scotland. I would love to have gone with him, but I couldn't afford it, so I saw him off at the station. He shot 73 round the championship course, and Raymond Oppenheimer (one of the English selectors) came up to him and said: "Who are you? Where do you come from?" Tony replied: "I come from Scunthorpe, and they call me Jacklin." "Well, you'll be playing for England tomorrow," he was told, and the first we knew of it, was when we read the local evening paper in Scunthorpe, and saw he was playing for England against the Continent.'

Tony enjoyed his golf with his father and their relationship. Now, he still enjoys his company, but acknowledges their differences: 'My old man is a great bloke – he's a good mate of mine. I like him and love him, but he's never been prepared to take a chance in his life. His security is in his everyday habit, his routine, and I've never known him do anything on the spur of the moment.

'I once took him to Australia, New Zealand and back through America. It was three weeks of time changes and bloody turmoil for him. He got back, shook hands, said thanks for the trip – it was really fantastic, I enjoyed it – but please don't ask me again.

'When I was young I don't think I was ever naughty, but I was an arrogant little sod and sometimes on the golf course my father would thump me. I always thought I knew better than he did – which I did. It used to aggravate me when I was standing over a shot and he would say, keep your head down, take it nice and slow. I'd say, Dad, I've already thought of that – leave me alone. He'd call me a cheeky bugger and thump me on the ear. He was always wanting to help, with the best will in the world.

'Once I got better than he was, he stopped. He has never meddled in my life since I became independent.

'When I was 13, I got my first handicap of 18 and won the first four competitions I entered. By the end of the year, I was pulled to 12 handicap, I was a bloody good player at 13. I used to get very nervous when I played in competitions, so that I had to have an egg whipped up in milk, because I couldn't eat before I played. I just wanted to be good, to be better than anyone else; that's what competition is about, beating other people.

'Whatever happens when you win a tournament, you lie in bed that night and say to yourself, well I waxed everybody today. That week, you were the best.

'I grew up to become a good golfer and it was all due to me, not to my parents. My Dad introduced me to the game, and they both encouraged me to play, but I had to go out and earn the money to do anything that I wanted to do in golf.

'The paper round brought in 10 shillings a week. On Saturdays, I worked for an auctioneer in the market and earned another 10 shillings, until I discovered a quicker way of making money, which was potato picking–and I could earn 12 shillings a day doing that. I also did some beating for a shoot. I did morning scrumping round the golf course looking for golf balls, because I couldn't afford to buy them. I spent all my money on golf, on little trips away to play competitively.

'I hated school and I left at 15 to become an apprentice fitter in the steel-works, because Mum and Dad said there was no money in being a golf professional. I got to work at 7.30 am, and filed lumps of steel standing at a bench all day, it was awful. You could spend three or four days working on one bit of steel–it would be 100th of an inch out, and a fellow would chuck it away and say, start again. I got £3 11s 3d a week for that.

'I had one hour for lunch, and I would rush through my meal in 10 minutes, then cycle three miles to the golf club, have 15 minutes practice and cycle back in time to clock in again. I packed in that job after a year.

'I went to work in a local Solicitor's office–a member of the golf club, Eric Kemp, said he would give me a job, and he paid me £6 a week, and I had nearly every afternoon off to play golf, which was great.

'But it wasn't what I wanted. Really I was the black sheep of the family. I didn't want to stay close to home and do what was expected of me, I wanted to become a professional golfer.

'One day, I saw a job advertised for a professional in Bakersfield, California, and I applied for it but I was turned down. I was prepared to go anywhere. Then I applied for a job as an assistant at Potters Bar Golf Club in Middlesex, and Bill Shankland, the professional, wanted me to go and see him. I hadn't told Dad I'd written, but I asked him to come down with me to the interview, and said I would only take the job if he thought it was all right.

'We went down and met Bill Shankland who was then 53, strong as a bull and a terrific character. You couldn't help being impressed with him, especially when you came from up in the sticks. He said he had had 30 assistants while he'd been a professional, that I would earn £6 a week, plus half of what I could make teaching and playing. My Dad was happy and I went into the job.

'When I first came down it was all great. I thought when I came to the big smoke that everyone in the world was as nice as pie. I had marvellous digs with a Mr and Mrs Baker in Potters Bar for £3 15s a week, which included three meals a day and doing everything for me. Originally I went for two weeks, while I looked around for somewhere permanent–I stayed for seven years.

'I arrived on the 1st January, 1962. I remember I had a grey suit that I got from my cousin, two pairs of slacks, a few shirts, and everything was in one suitcase. I had a fiver, and that was it.

'There was three feet of snow on the ground, so Shanko (Bill Shankland) said to me, you'd better go back home. I said, I can't, this is it, I've left home. It was like St Moritz, and for the first week I played snooker.

'Then the honeymoon was over and I began to see the other side of Shanko. After three months at Potters Bar, I applied for a job with Keith Hockey at Muswell Hill. Shanko didn't know, until Keith rang up and asked if I was any good. "He's bloody useless," he said. Then he yelled at me, "What are you doing applying for other jobs? I should sack you– you're an arrogant little bastard."

'And I was. I was cocky. I always knew I wanted to be a player and not in a shop. He had a business to run and I could see his point–it was up to us to do as we were told.

'At the time, so far as I was concerned, he was a bastard and he did everything he could to make my life miserable. Nothing I ever did was right: the shop wasn't clean enough; I was never there long enough; whatever I did, there was something wrong; if I played well in a tournament, I was lucky.

'Another of the assistants there was Denis Scanlan. If Shanko had been particularly rotten to us, then out of spite and to get even, we would take the shirts out of the packages in the shop, wear them to go out at night and then fold them up and put them back the next morning before Shanko came in.

'Shanko was great in spending a lot of time with me, and with all his assistants, on the practice ground, which not enough professionals bother to do. I learned to pick his mind in golf terms.

'Within three months of being there, I won the Middlesex Assistants' Championship and came third in the senior event. I improved and got better all the time. In 1963, I was runner-up in the Gor-Ray Assistants' Championship and finished high in a number of other tournaments, and I won the Henry Cotton Rookie of the Year prize of £100.

'I loathed teaching. I would go out to teach taking only a dozen balls,

12

so that most of the hour was spent picking them up. I would rather have given them the fee not to come than give the lesson. The members were great – they were very nice to me, it was a Jewish club and I had a great rapport with them.

'One thing that motivated me more than anything was Shanko's Austin Westminster in the car park. I said to myself – one day, I'm going to park my car next to his, and mine will make his look like a heap of tin. I did it. I drove in my Rolls-Royce in 1970 and put it next to his car. There was no satisfaction. It was lost in having gone on to bigger and better things – your outlook broadens and you see how you were motivated by things because of circumstances.

'Certainly Shanko and I had a personality clash. I used to reckon that if I could have shot him and got away with it, I would have done so. I hated him that much. If I could have pulled the trigger and no one knew it was me – I would have been happy. I lay awake at night because I was so unhappy – he made me feel inferior. I was a bit arrogant, but I always thought I was good, and to do well, you have to think that.

'The only thing that made me stick it was that I had too much pride to go home, and without a reference I couldn't get a decent job. The main line to the North goes past Potters Bar, and there were so many times I wished I was on that sodding train. But I couldn't see myself knocking on the door, saying, I'm back, I'm home; it would have been like admitting defeat.

'Shanko was a good businessman, a good golf professional for Potters Bar, a darned good player and teacher, but a hard man on his assistants.

'Unquestionably, being there, probably made me. I couldn't have had a better grounding. It was like doing the National Service that I never had to do. It hardened me, it really did, but I wouldn't go through it again.'

Bill Shankland still gives the impression of a large, strong man. He comes from Australia, and he was a Rugby League International from 1926. When he toured Britain in 1928 and 1929, he signed up with the highest fee ever paid – £1,000 – to play for Warrington. He also used to box: 'I could be very cruel and spiteful, but I'm a softie really,' he says.

Alongside the other sports, he became a professional golfer, taking an assistant's job at West Lancs Golf Club, and then in 1934 he became the professional at Haydock Park Golf Club. In the 1939 Open Championship at St Andrews, he finished third.

After the war, in 1947, he was third in the Open Championship at Hoylake, where Fred Daly won: 'I had a very good chance of winning, then in the final round, I took six, being in a bunker on the 16th hole. I felt sick for three months after.' In 1951, he tied third in the Open Championship at Royal Portrush in Ireland, won by Max Faulkner, who, as it turned out, was the last Briton before Tony Jacklin to win the title.

Bill Shankland remembers the early days of Tony Jacklin: 'When he first came to me at Potters Bar he was a brash young lad of 16½ but he was a personable, good-looking chap. I had four other assistants and he took his place–there were no favourites.

'He didn't like my putting my thumbs on him. Although he says I was, I was never tough, I was firm. I'm a softie really, though I could be hard if the boys didn't do their job.

'One day, he said, could you have a look at me Sir? He didn't want me to look at him the first month–he thought he was God–which is a good thing in golf as it's a selfish game and you've got to think a bit of yourself. About time, I said, then I took him out, changed his grip, which was weak– he fell in with it and started to blossom.

'I'm not going to say that at that moment I knew he was going to be good. But after he had been with me about 18 months, I could see it, but I couldn't have said he would win two Opens.

'I don't think there was a personality clash–I've always been a very friendly person. He was sometimes a devil and was mixing with the wrong fellows at tournaments. Once he went into a club in Scotland with a girl, where no woman had ever been, which was a bit naughty. I told him, I have a good name in the business, you behave yourself or I'll fire you, and then you'll never get a job anywhere.

'He was probably scared of me sometimes and felt like going home, because I could be tough on him. But he's got much to thank me for–even the fact that I was a little bit tough–it did him good. No doubt it was the making of him. It's easy for young fellows to go off the rails, especially when they do well.

'He became a very good player. He's very strong. I could lift a chair with one hand, and he could too, he used to do it easily. He strengthened his hands, and put on about a stone and a half while he was with me. He was always miles ahead of the others, with a tenacity of purpose, and he was single-minded in the mould of all champions.

'I still say Tony's one of the best putters in the world. You've got to be a good putter to do as well as he did. It's never been heard of to win the two Opens in a year.

'You can help to make fellows, and I'm sure I made Tony in the first year he was with me. You've got to initially mould them. I'm very proud to say I had much to do with giving him a start and a good foundation.'

While Tony was an assistant at Potters Bar, he and another assistant, Richard Emery at Mill Hill, who was one of the best players in the area, would put money on the line that they didn't possess, as a wager against anyone who would play them.

'We played a lot of challenge matches at £50 a time,' says Richard, 'and we never lost. It was a lot of money. I was earning £2 10s a week.

'The first time I ever heard of Tony, was at the 1962 Middlesex Assistants' Championship. I'd produced two pretty good scores and he beat me into second place by about seven shots.

'I could foresee him doing what he did, because he was such a great

14

Top left: *Tony at 4½ months old, November 1944.* Top right: *Early spoils. Scunthorpe Open Day Cup and Elsham Open Day Cup, aged 13, 1957.* Centre: *Tony and his parents with the Lincolnshire Open Trophy aged 16.* Right: *Tony and first boss Bill Shankland shared a love-hate relationship.*

player in his early days, and he had so much confidence. He knew he was good – he was bound to make it. Also, he basically wanted to make himself into a successful, rich person.

'In the early days, I could at times play as well as he played, but I didn't really, in my heart, feel I could do it all the time as he certainly did. He was cocky, that's why he was good. I could never stand on the tee and think, who on earth is going to beat me, as Tony did. I could certainly see he would win an Open within a few years – it was no surprise to me at all.'

Tony continued working at Potters Bar and playing as many tournaments as he could, but Bill Shankland was reluctant to let him go away to play. After a year, the club members chipped into a fund to provide Tony's wages, and a pool to draw on – handed out by Bill Shankland – for tournament expenses, should he need them.

'I played the 1963 Open at Lytham,' says Tony, 'and finished in 30th place making £56 13s 4d. I played other tournaments where I made enough money to cover myself. In 1964 I went to the Open at St Andrews, but failed to get through the pre-qualifying, which was the only time I ever claimed expenses, and they were about £25.

'In the summer of 1964 I was working my arse off for Shankland. For several months I was the only assistant and I never had a day off. I was working 12 to 14 hours a day, doing the books, cleaning clubs, doing repairs, scrubbing the floor, cleaning his car, giving lessons. And so far as he was concerned, I couldn't do anything right.

'The explosion came in September. Shanko and I had some bloody up and downers, until inevitably the bubble burst. Finally, in floods of tears, I told him to stick the job, that I wouldn't work there for £100 a week. He said, fine, that's it. And I said, I'm off, although I didn't know where I was going – I had £343 in the bank.'

The man who had been mainly responsible for raising Tony's financial pool, so that he could play tournaments, was the President of the golf club, Johnnie Rubens. When Tony said he was leaving, Bill Shankland telephoned Johnnie.

'The following morning,' says Tony, 'I was still there working out a week's notice and Johnnie Rubens turned up at the club. He asked me to go out and play. "How are things?" he said. I blurted it all out and said I couldn't work for Shankland any longer.

'Johnnie said he understood, and that the club would like me to stay and use the facilities of the club without being responsible to Shankland. I could teach and play with members and keep what I made.

'So I stayed on, although I didn't play or teach at the club because I felt it was wrong and that I was encroaching on Shankland's domain. We didn't fall out – I still talked to him – but I came and went as I pleased.'

Johnnie Rubens, a man who made his money in property, remembers his first impressions of Tony Jacklin: 'When he won the Middlesex Assistants' Championship by a huge margin, playing with second-hand clubs after he'd been with us only a few weeks–that set us on fire–this terrific unknown youngster. I'd seen plenty of assistants–they all hit the ball for miles and looked marvellous when you played with them, and then they didn't do anything.

'In 1963, we decided to send Tony to the Open Championship at Royal Lytham and had a whip round, which raised about £100. On the Monday following the Championship, a close friend of mine, Lou Freedman, a Vice-President of the PGA, rang me and said he'd been talking with fellows such as Dai Rees and Michael Bonallack and they had told him this youngster Jacklin had tremendous potential and should be encouraged.

'So here's a youngster in the shop with potential and you encourage him–that's how it started. I sat and talked to him and realised (talking from hindsight) that he was in a different class, in that he could make the scores. I wasn't such a great judge of professional golf, but I realised he had a quality the others didn't possess.

'I found he hated being in the shop, selling golf balls, clubs, and giving lessons–people said he was the worst teacher they ever had. All he wanted to do was play tournament golf. That to me was good, what I liked to hear. He just wanted to be a fine golfer. So we organised an expenses fund for him.

'Unless you're ambitious, you don't get anywhere. He had ambitions, dreams, drive, talent and intelligence, you need them all. I smelt it in Tony.

'I used to go and watch him at tournaments because I had a personal interest. You feel a satisfaction in seeing something develop that you have helped to create. We gave him the opportunity, which very few assistants have, to get out of the shop. He stood on his own feet financially and he started making a living, which was the object of the exercise. It was a gamble that came off.'

2: The Making of a Tournament Golfer

WHEN TONY REMAINED attached to Potters Bar Golf Club in the autumn of 1964, the President of the club, Johnnie Rubens, asked him what he was going to do in the winter months. Tony had little idea, until Johnnie offered to lend him £200 to go to South Africa. He grasped the opportunity, obtained a further loan from Dunlop of £200, which he added to his own £343 in the bank, and set off on an eight-week tour of South Africa.

'I found the unaccustomed nap on the greens over there very hard. In eight weeks, I only made about two cuts and I won £35 in prize money. I spent £600 on air fares and expenses. It was my first trip away from home and I felt terrible when I returned with only £143 in the world and a golf game – but it was a great investment.

'The Potters Bar members were always there in the back of my mind – they supported me in the best way – which was to be there if I needed them.

'In 1965, I did reasonably well in tournaments in Britain. I had my first trip to America, when I qualified for the Carling tournament at Pleasant Valley where I played well to finish 30th, winning $1,000 and beating Arnold Palmer by one shot.

'The last day of the Carling, there was a rain-out, so that play was cancelled and we had to stay an extra day. That meant I would arrive home for the Gor-Ray Assistants' Championship at Coombe Hill, Surrey, on the first day of the tournament. I contacted the PGA Secretary, John Bywaters, to ask him to put me out last, which he did.

'I began with a round of 74, then needed a birdie on the 36th hole to qualify for the last two rounds, which I got. Then with two 68s I caught up 10 shots on the leaders, birdieing the 72nd hole to force a play-off against Sean Hunt and David Butler. I won with a birdie on the first hole, to become Assistants' Champion.'

By the end of the year, Tony had won over £1,000 which put him 11th in the Order of Merit. And an important event had happened in his life – he had met his future wife, Vivien, a Belfast girl, when he was playing the Jeyes tournament in June, at Bangor, Northern Ireland.

'I met Viv in a pub and asked her to have a drink with me. She refused and said she was going out with a fellow in the band. I said what about tomorrow? She agreed – and that was it, she was the girl for me. I went home to continue playing the tournaments and it was costing me a fortune in 'phone calls.

'In November I went over to see her father – it was all done properly – and asked him if we could get engaged. I was very nervous and he's the easiest guy in the world. He agreed that we should. I felt that once you meet the right person you should get on with it.

'Then I returned home and went to see Johnnie Rubens. I told him that I was going to South Africa again in the winter, because I thought I could do better than the previous year, but before I went I wanted to pay back the £200 I owed him. He was surprised, as I think he had written it off. He asked me what it would cost to go, and I said another £600. He sat down and wrote me a cheque for £100, telling me to forget what I owed him.

'I went to South Africa, won £1,000 and tied the last tournament at Kimberley with Harold Henning. It was all a very gradual process but I felt it was as it was supposed to be.

'At the beginning of the 1966 season in Britain, I started well, coming third in the Penfold, third in the Martini, fifth in the Schweppes. I had decided I wanted to get married and I went over to see Viv in Belfast, and said, let's get married tomorrow. She said it wasn't practical and we decided to make it in a month's time, after the Blaxnit tournament near Belfast. I told her that I would make £1,000 in the next month, which was a lot of money, but I managed to do it.

'I went over and won the Blaxnit tournament at Malone, and then on 30th May we were married. I was 21, Viv 23, and everyone had told us that we should wait. But the majority of great golfers have all been married very young–it's an important part of growing up–maturing and having responsibility.

'We spent our honeymoon at a London Airport hotel, because I was playing nearby in the Daks tournament, which I led after three rounds and then blew it to finish seventh, as I was lacking in experience.

'Before we got married, I told Viv–and it was difficult to tell a girl when you're 21 and you've fallen in love with her–that I would always love her, but golf came first and that's how it was.

'She was sensible enough to realise what I meant. It didn't mean that I didn't love her–it meant that no human being could take pride of place over golf at that point, but if anyone could, then she was first in line.

'Marriage made me knuckle under–it was the greatest thing that ever happened. They write movies about what we did, and they don't compare to the real life adventure of travelling the world with a set of golf clubs, a suitcase, and the woman you love–it was fantastic.

'I always told Viv we'd be loaded and have everything, and she would laugh at me. I told her we'd have so much, nothing would matter.

'I think everyone has dreams to do certain things but often they get side-tracked on the way. The people who succeed are too single-minded to be side-tracked and never lose sight of their ultimate goal. The dedicated ones, those who really care, are going to make it. And at the end of it, the crazy thing is that you've gained the respect of all the others–so it's worth it. You're looked up to by those who didn't try so hard, and they say, well I could have, but . . . the guy who succeeds didn't say "but".

'Viv has been fantastic. She always maintains that I would have made it, with or without her. That may or may not be true. The point is, that having had her to share the whole thing has made it far more pleasant.

'It's like going to see a fantastic sight – the first thing you want to do is to share it with someone you love, who is close to you. The same as if you have a great meal – than it's, ooh, taste that, isn't it good?

'One real joy is that she has been able to share the whole bit and has built up a terrific experience in the same things. So many things don't need saying between us. It's very fortunate she came along at the right time and that we get on so well. We never argue, which is great. Sometimes I would call her from America and say, come over this afternoon, and she would hop on a 'plane and arrive – that's what it is all about. How could anyone put a price on something like that? It was all part of the whole thing and Viv has been great all the way through.'

Vivien Jacklin has very definitely grown, matured and expanded her horizons alongside Tony. She is a fairly reserved person: 'In Ireland no one goes up and kisses anyone else, you don't peck people on the cheek – English people do that,' she says, but she immediately makes you feel welcome, and at ease, and she is an excellent hostess.

As a youngster she played netball for Ireland – her family were much involved in sport and she was a sports enthusiast. She went to work at 15 as an accounting machine operator, to earn money to keep her two clever brothers at school. Her father worked as a stores labourer and her mother was an accomplished needlewoman.

They were a close family: 'I think closeness as a family,' says Vivien, 'and your attitude to your husband, depend on how you were brought up. My father never came in from work without finding his meal on the table. My mother felt her duty to her family came first. She said, if you're a woman your place is in the home, you must do all the domestic duties – the man must not do anything.

'Personally, I don't see anything wrong in the woman going out to work if she has nothing at home to hold her back. But I prefer to stay home, and anyway I've never had the talent for anything else.

'I always felt I should put my husband first and that I'd got to be able to lead his life. I always set out his clothes for him in the morning, having pressed them first, and I travelled everywhere with him. I've always let Tony make the decisions, because he's not the sort of man who wants a wife who makes decisions.

'I didn't really know what to expect when we got married. He said it wasn't going to be a bed of roses. He didn't mean to be offensive when he said golf came first. I'd have been disappointed if he hadn't felt that way because he had a career and he had to do something with it, and that is acceptable.

'In a quiet way I suppose I'm ambitious, in that I want everything to go

20

right, everyone to be happy and content with life. My ambition is to be good at what I do. Life is never dull with Tony and I've always enjoyed his ambition. I wish I were more like him and could go out and succeed, but it's not in my personality.

'I've tried to help him do the right thing and I think it's worth making sacrifices in order to succeed. You've got to sacrifice a lot to be great and I would never take away from Tony his urge to succeed.

'I don't think he's selfish; everyone is selfish to a point and anyone ambitious has to be a bit selfish – everything has to revolve around him to make it work. It is self-centred, but it's no big deal.

'I knew right away when we met that Tony was right for me – we both felt the same. I don't know what Tony would do if he had someone with some interest other than him. He needs a woman to devote herself to him and I enjoy that.

'When I met Tony I knew nothing about golf and I had no idea what he could do or how good he was. Actually, it wasn't until we had been married for about a year that I began to think he would make a living at it.

'I didn't pay any attention when he said we would have a big house, a nice car, and that within five years he would buy me a mink coat. I never had money and the lack of it didn't bother me.

'I have made everything as easy as I could for him, but when I hear husbands say, I owe it all to my wife – that to me is absolute nonsense. You can help in little things, be quiet and calm, but a man does most of it himself. He must have the talent and brains or he would never succeed.

'I've never pushed Tony, because a person who is going to be great doesn't need to be pushed. In golf, it's no good being an ambitious wife, as it's the husbands who have to play the shots.'

By the end of the 1966 season Tony had won £2,700 and was fifth in the Order of Merit. He became the youngest British professional to compete in the Canada Cup (now World Cup) when he teamed up to play with Peter Alliss in Japan in November.

Tony invested £1,100 in two air tickets from Japan to Australia, New Zealand, and right round the Far East, where he and Vivien spent the next five months.

'We had a great time,' says Viv, 'we'd never been anywhere before or seen anything, and we really enjoyed it. We would hitch-hike between tournaments and I would caddie. Tony played quite well. He tied Bob Charles in a tournament and then won the New Zealand PGA Championship in a play-off against Dutchman, Martin Roesink.

'Then we went to Australia where he finished third in a tournament before Christmas. We spent several weeks there and during that time Tony got an invitation to play in the Masters at Augusta the following April, because Neil Coles didn't want to fly and was giving up his place, and Tony was next in line. Peter Thomson told Tony he wouldn't like it, he wouldn't do well and he shouldn't go. But Tony said, I'm going, that's it.

'We went on around the Far East to Manila, Singapore, Kuala Lumpur, Bangkok–where he came third in a tournament–and Hong Kong. As Tony made money, we spent it. One time we threw out all our old things and each got a new wardrobe–dresses, handbags, shoes, shirts and suits.'

From Hong Kong the Jacklins travelled to Augusta, Georgia, for the Masters in April: 'I played with Bobby Nichols in the first two rounds,' says Tony, 'and sometime later he told me he thought I was going to win, he'd never seen anyone play like it, such great, inspired stuff. I played with Arnold Palmer in the third round, and at one stage I was leading the tournament; Palmer shot 73, I shot 69, which put me three behind the lead. I had no experience and shot 77 in the last round to finish in 16th place– but it was my finest achievement at that stage.

'To me, America was the end of the rainbow, it was where I felt I should be. At the beginning of the week at Augusta, no one knew who I was, they thought I was an amateur. At the end of the week, I had made my mark.'

Tony returned for an impressive 1967 British season. He won the Pringle tournament, making up 10 shots in the last two rounds and having six birdies in the last nine holes. He came fifth in the Open Championship at Hoylake, won by Roberto de Vicenzo. He went to the Canadian Open and finished 11th; at the Carling tournament in Toronto he was in joint 7th place. He became managed by American, Mark McCormack–which at that time was becoming recognised as a sign of a promising future.

Shortly after he won the Dunlop Masters at Royal St George's, Sandwich, in spectacular style. He opened with a fine 69; followed with a mediocre 74, and then blazed a trail with a 67, and a record-breaking 64– the previous record of 65 having been set up 33 years earlier by Henry Cotton. The 64 included a dramatic hole-in-one at the 163-yard 16th hole, where his seven iron shot went into the cup, the first hole-in-one to be seen by millions, live on television. That round gave him a three-shot victory.

Tony played in his first Ryder Cup match in Houston, Texas, where he was one of the most successful of the British team, winning two matches and halving one. He ended the season by qualifying through American school at West Palm Beach to give him a ticket to the United States PGA Tour. He needed to score 68, 68, in the last two rounds to secure his place. His winnings for that year were around the high mark of £10,000. Tony Jacklin was becoming a name.

It was at this juncture that Tony proclaimed: 'I want to be the best golfer in the world. I want to win all the major championships of the world and become a millionaire. You've always got to have an ambition, otherwise life's not worth living.'

Tony and Vivien Jacklin joined the US Tour in January 1968. 'I remember,' says Viv, 'that a red-haired Press man asked Tony what he expected to achieve in America his first year. Tony said, I'm going to win a tournament, and the fellow laughed and said, you don't know what you're talking about. Tony was quite positive–he never doubted it.

'We started travelling with Tom and Jean Weiskopf, and Bert and Linda Yancey, and it was all fun, we had a lot in common.

'Tony played quite well at the start in California and was always in the money. Then when the Tour moved to Florida, where he likes the courses, he had nine straight rounds all under 70 and won the Governor of Florida's trophy.

'At the Citrus Open he tied 4th; at the Pensacola Open he came second; the following week he played super golf and he won at Jacksonville. The red-haired Press man was there and congratulated him – he said he was amazed. I thought it was going to happen from the build-up to it. At Jacksonville there was a huge flashing scoreboard with all the statistics, and it was very exciting to see that Tony was the first British golfer to win a tournament in America for nearly 50 years.'

The Jacklins' friend, Johnnie Rubens from Potters Bar, was in America and flew up to Jacksonville for the last round. Tony was paired with Arnold Palmer who made a charge to draw level with him, but then dropped back to tie seventh with a 73, while Tony's 71, added to his previous rounds of 68, 65, 69, gave him the title by two shots over five Americans tied behind him.

The Jacksonville victory put him third on the US money list with nearly £20,000 that he had won in 12 weeks. It was also the first four-round PGA tournament to have ever been won by a Briton, the last win being by Ted Ray in 1920, when he won the US Open, which is a national Open event.

'I played very well all that year,' says Tony. 'The whole thing was new and very exciting. No one had a better time in the history of the world, because from 1966 I did everything and won it all with Vivien. All the decisions were right and we made them all happen. I could see what I had to do and I went out and did it.

'Together we went round the world and they were three years of playing golf and having a good time doing it. Everything was a risk – we got married, borrowed money, and they were the greatest days, the most fun I ever had. There was the self-satisfaction of taking the bull by the horns. I won Jacksonville and never looked back.'

Tony's continued good form meant that by the end of the season he had amassed an amazing £40,000 in winnings, which was unheard of for a young British player. Having lived with his parents in Scunthorpe, Tony now invested in a house at Elsham in Lincolnshire. He bought Vivien that mink coat and an Aston Martin for himself.

But the season was to finish on rather a sour note. In the last British tournament, the Piccadilly World Match-Play, Tony had gained a coveted place. He and Brian Huggett were the only British players.

In the first round at Wentworth, played over 36 holes of the West course, Tony beat Lee Trevino with a good 4 and 3 victory, while Gary Player beat Australian, Peter Thomson, by a resounding 8 and 7 margin. In the second round, Player and Jacklin met.

The weather that week was miserably wet, but there were huge crowds who were obviously hoping for a British victory. Jacklin took the lead for the first time against Player in the afternoon, when he went ahead at the third hole, and then went two up as Player failed to get a par at the fifth hole. Then Jacklin dropped five shots in four holes and became two down, which he remained until the 16th hole, where he birdied to get one back. At the long, par 5 17th he had another birdie to square the match.

At the 495-yard 18th hole, in spite of wet, heavy conditions, Player was on the front edge of the green with two huge shots. Jacklin had to wedge out from trees on the right, and his ball almost plugged on the green, slightly inside Player. Player putted to four feet; Jacklin left his 10 feet short, but sank his next for a par five. 'I was standing with my glove in my hand, getting ready to shake hands, and Gary missed his putt,' recalls Tony.

'When we were playing the 18th, the referee, Arthur Crawley-Boevey, had asked me whether we should continue the match if we halved that hole, because it was raining and getting dark. I had said I thought we could. But Gary, who had just missed from four feet, said we should never have played the 18th (36th) and we certainly couldn't go on.'

Jacklin and Player returned the next day, but the rain was torrential and play was completely washed out. The following morning a large crowd followed the two golfers to the first tee, their 37th hole. Jacklin drove well and with an excellent second, was 30 feet short of the flag. Player hooked his second 70 yards short, where he claimed casual water, dropped out and played a fine wedge to 10 feet.

Tony says: 'I putted up five feet short—a bad putt. He hit his 10 footer and it went into the centre of the hole. As it went in, he turned round and said to a guy in the crowd, "You said miss it, miss it." Then he went on for two minutes lecturing the gallery about how he was a visitor to the country, they should have more respect, give him a chance, he was only doing a job.

'Meanwhile, I had a five-foot putt to make, and two minutes of listening to Gary is a long time. I missed my putt. I'm not saying I would have made it, but Gary hadn't helped. Really it was bad manners—whether it was classed as gamesmanship I don't know. But he won the match and went on to win the event.'

Tony's bunker play at Lytham was the corner-stone of his victory.

Tony drives in his final round at Lytham.

The Cup that cheers: Tony and Vivien greet new friend.

*Tony and US Open trophy
at PGA dinner 1970.*

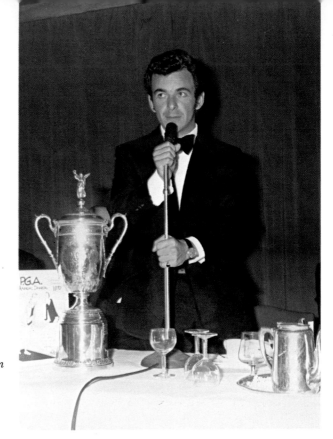

*Pro-celebrity golf 1977. From
left: Bing Crosby, Tony,
Sean Connery and Johnny
Miller with caddies at
Gleneagles for BBC TV.*

3: Royal Lytham and St Annes

TONY JACKLIN had a dream. Tony Jacklin made it happen. It was at Royal Lytham and St Annes that a dark-haired, 25-year-old lad from Scunthorpe, Lincolnshire, strode confidently down the final hole in the 1969 Open Championship – after his drive had split the middle of the fairway.

Everyone watching held their breath, instinctively knowing they were witnessing sporting history in the making. A beautifully played iron to the heart of the green, two more putts, and the whole arena erupted with joy, acclaiming the first British golfer to win the Open for 18 years.

And what a champion he was – young, good-looking with a magnetic personality, and a great talent. The noise swelled, if you weren't crying, then there was a big lump in your throat, and the strains of 'For He's A Jolly Good Fellow' heightened the emotion of the moment.

Tony came to the Press tent and the Press rose to clap him with an extra dimension of warmth and affection – they too were captivated.

Tony responded: 'Well I just don't know what to say really. Today I thought I'd try to forget it was the Open Championship altogether. I tried to play each shot as it came, tried not to panic. I was so nervous, really, I was never as nervous in my life as I have been these last two days. I didn't know what to do with myself – sit around – I was blaming everybody for putting me off too late, expecting everyone to start at six o'clock so that I could play at nine, rather than hang about all morning.

'I feel wonderful about winning – really it hasn't sunk in yet. Undoubtedly it's the greatest moment of my life. It was one of my main ambitions to win the British Open, I just never thought it would come so soon and I feel very grateful that it has. It makes all the travelling that I've done over the past couple of years in America worthwhile.'

Tony's dream had started a long time before that Open Championship and he had worked hard to make it happen: 'If you have a dream and it's pure, if you have an imagination to go with it, and if you believe in yourself beyond all else, then nothing can stop you. You must believe you can do it. Only a very few have a picture of what is going to happen and then go out with the purposefulness to achieve it.

'When I practised as a kid, I found it boring to stand out there all day hitting golf balls – you have to figure out some way of making yourself do it. I imagined I was being watched over by Ben Hogan. I picked him because he was the epitome of perfection with regard to striking a golf ball, so that unless the shot was perfect I knew he was going to turn up his nose. I had to make a perfect swing every time, and every swing I made he would comment on. Or, I would try to imagine that I had a particular shot to hit to the last green in an Open Championship.

'You're dreaming then. But if you can attain a standard of play that takes you from the ordinary into a higher class you start thinking in terms of winning a tournament. If you win a tournament, then some players are happy with that; in their heart of hearts they really don't want any more–they don't want to be more than just a good player, because of the pressure. There are numerous players with more talent than some of the actual winners, but they don't want the pressure. It's sad. While you're doing it, you may as well go the whole bloody hog.

'Think of a guy like Brian Barnes who's a good mate of mine, who has all the talent necessary to win the British and US Opens; he's a better player potentially than, say, Hubert Green. I think of Tom Weiskopf, who has won an Open–I'm criticising now, which is easy–but these two guys, Weiskopf and Barnes, are both solid putters and they have no particular hang-ups, other than that they just seem to lose their rag. If it's going all right, okay–and if it's not, sod it.

'There are many ingredients in winning, obviously you must be a good player, but you've got to be lucky as well. I played better in the Open at Muirfield where I lost, than in the one at Lytham where I won. You must be lucky in respect of no one taking a run at you. I really didn't do anything startling the last day at Lytham, but neither did anyone else. Johnny Miller didn't shoot 63 in the last round as he did when he won the 1973 US Open–neither did Nicklaus come in with a 65–and that matters.

'I can remember that the toughest job I had when I won the British and US Opens, was not thinking about the prize-giving ceremony and receiving the trophy–not letting my mind wander ahead. I was always saying to myself: come back, bring it back, stay here, now, in the present, and don't wander ahead wondering what you are going to say, or how marvellous it would be if . . . that's two hours away, come back, you've got a 15-footer here–make it, think about that.

'And it's tough. That was difficult, really bloody difficult. No kidding– it's not romantic. But then it's such a marvellous prize.

'During the years I played very well in the Open Championship–I was never far away from the top, I was always there with a chance. The better player you are, the more you are around, and the odds are that you're going to be successful one time or another. You can't just be there one time in 10, because when it comes to the crunch–those last nine holes– you either do it or you don't, you've got it or you haven't, call it what you like, courage, bottle or guts.

'I like Open courses, I really do. In 1967 I played well in the Open at Hoylake, where Roberto de Vicenzo won, and I finished fifth. At Carnoustie in 1968 where Gary Player won, I finished 16th and shot 80 in the last round. I played some of the most superb golf I've ever played but I didn't have enough experience, I didn't believe I was that good.

Above left: *It's all mine. Tony lays his first putt dead on the final green at Royal Lytham.* Above right: *Tony and Bob Charles after the last putt. Did Charles use gamesmanship on the final tee?* Below left: *Champagne like success is an acquired taste. Mark McCormack and the law share the moment.* Below right: *Tony waves to the crowds on his way to the prize-giving. Roberto de Vicenzo is on his right.*

'The greatest experience a child can have is to travel, to see the world. In my terms when it came to those golfing situations, then the experience had to be gained by going and playing in America, playing with lots of fellows to see how good they are, whether they're better than you; saying to yourself, this guy has won two tournaments and I don't think he's any better than I am. You must be honest with yourself.

'It all boils down to the fact that you've got to see it first-hand before you can make that type of assessment. You must believe that on your day you're as good as any of them and you can't gain that experience being confined in one area. Like Neil Coles for instance, whom I would pick as being a really marvellous player–he's got everything. But I believe the choice he has made regarding travel–he won't fly for whatever reason, also the fact that he sits around for several months a year building boats– that has to hurt when it comes to the ultimate crux like an Open. Then he probably never really believes enough in himself. There's no substitute for grinding it out around the world.

'The fact is that when you're young, on top of it all and wanting to make it all happen, you purely and simply know that you have the ability to get the ball round the course in less strokes than anyone else. Then you make it happen by looking, watching, doing, and you don't analyse it. The reason Severiano Ballesteros does so well is his natural flair, his ability to want to be the best to hit the golf ball a certain way, and his appeal to the public. People start to make it more difficult by analysing it.

'Imagination motivates you to win. But why golfers should get so much recognition for winning I don't know. You could be a great mathematician, a genius, and people don't write about you. Freud and Einstein were much deeper, they were far more worthy of recognition than Hogan or Nicklaus. Their impact was far greater on the world.

'But to win you must have a dream. You've got to make that dream a reality, and that's the difficult part. Obviously loads of people have dreams but some people seem to make them happen.'

A few weeks before the Open Championship, Tony was dreaming only of home. He was grinding it out on the American tour and he had missed the cut in four tournaments, and was coming up for missing it for the fifth time in a period of six weeks. Playing the second round of a tournament in Dallas, Texas, with his wife Vivien following faithfully on the sidelines, he suddenly walked over to her and said, 'Book us on the next 'plane– we're off home.' The Jacklins got on the next flight to England and sped northwards to Scunthorpe. 'You just can't imagine how pleased I was to be back. I kept saying to Vivien, do you realise that's English grass, those are English trees, this is the English countryside. I know it sounds stupid, but that's just how strongly I felt about being home.'

Tony filled his lungs with Lincolnshire air for a couple of weeks, before returning to America to sharpen up his game for what was to be the greatest moment of his life.

Open Championship week arrived: 'I played it as it came–I can't remember the scores, I'm hopeless at things like that. You've got to hang loose a little bit and bide your time. You play as well as you can the first day and make a position. You don't go out on the first hole of a Championship and turn on concentration like a tap, you play with it, you're apprehensive at first, you get away with it and then on the fourth or fifth hole you may get into it. You're loose, you're keyed up, but early on you think of a good swing. You've already played the round 12 times the night before, whether you really wanted to or not, you have. You've possibly thought of the first shot you're going to hit–it's an important shot to you–and you've got to make a good pass at it.

'You work your way into winning. I treat it with the utmost respect. I would never say: I think I'll win. I always think something will happen to take it away if you are over-confident about anything. You must not get too complacent. I've never won without giving up all my time to that whole thing; it's there when you're eating dinner, brushing your teeth, it might even be sleeping in your mind, but it's always there. It's hard work, very hard work–and it takes a lot out of you.

'You've got it all within you. I remember when Bert Yancey lost the 1968 US Open to Lee Trevino. Afterwards, Arnold Palmer said to me, "I didn't think Yancey would win–he was talking too much." What do you mean, I asked? "He's trying to get rid of the pressure. But you can't talk, you've got to take it inside your gut." Palmer is right, things happen and you have to swallow hard, you have a knot in your stomach, and you've got to come to terms with yourself because that's how you earn your living. Some players can–a lot can't. That's why you have so few champions.'

In the first round of the 1969 Open Championship, Tony started in great style as he holed from 18 feet for a birdie two at the opening hole. He then single putted the 4th, 5th and 6th greens to go four under par after six holes. He came in with an excellent round of 68, to be tied with Yorkshireman Hedley Muscroft, two shots behind the left-handed New Zealander, Bob Charles, who was leading the field with a five under par 66–a new course record. After a reasonably steady second round 70, Tony was tied with his old mate Alex Caygill on 138, two behind Irishman, Christy O'Connor, and three shots back from Charles, whose 69 put him on 135.

The third day Tony produced a fine 70: 'The third round was a great round. I was in umpteen traps, and I got down in two shots every time–not coming out close, but to about eight or nine feet and holing the putts. I was hanging on and I was making the situation by what I was doing.' Tony also had a new sand-iron that week, because before the Championship began the Royal and Ancient had advised him not to use his old one as the grooves in it were possibly too deep to be legal. At the end of the day Tony was in the lead on 208–five under par; Charles who had taken 75 was tied on 210 with Christy O'Connor; one shot further back were Roberto de Vicenzo and Peter Thomson, followed on 213 by Jack Nicklaus and Brian Huggett. Tony had to cope with the coming hours – the evening and the morning before the biggest moment of his life.

'That night Viv and I stayed at home in the house that we were sharing with Bert and Linda Yancey. It's very difficult to explain how you feel at a golf tournament when you're playing very well. You're very keyed up then you come off the golf course and it's time to relax. But you can never totally relax because you have this thing on your mind all the time. You try to push it to one side but in something like the Open it is very difficult to do that. You occupy yourself with conversation on different aspects of life then any slack moment comes along and this thing jumps back out at you – how you're situated and what might happen tomorrow.

'I'd never taken sleeping pills much before that. I thought I would benefit from a good night's sleep – I didn't want to lay awake at three in the morning and wonder if . . . or whether . . . you can go through it a million times and it doesn't make any difference. What happens at the time is going to be the criteria. So I took a sleeping pill, fell asleep in the chair and Bert carried me up to bed, slipping me between the sheets around midnight. I woke at eight the next morning which was marvellous.

'But then you've still got to wait until nearly two o'clock to play and that is a bastard – trying to occupy your mind until then. It's all right as long as you're thinking about something else, if you're saying, oh there's a guy, there's a car, let's go for a drive and see some old castle or something – anything to take your mind off what you've got to do. You don't want to expend any of the energy you'll need later on.

'Then the time draws closer and it's time to go and warm up. You go and warm up and you feel this terrific pressure situation. Suddenly, it's tee-off time. Well, what happens now? What happens is, that you have to go out and think about every shot – there's no room for anything else. You say, I've got to concentrate for three seconds every shot, just be positive all the time, concentrate taking it back, and have a picture of where the ball is going. It's the normal everyday thing you say, that you're doing all the time, be positive, commit yourself, and do it. Whatever it takes – you goad yourself to do it.'

Playing with Bob Charles, Tony took command of the final round in great style. It was Charles who dropped a shot at the first, as Tony parred the first two holes, then sank a marvellous five-yard putt on the third green for a birdie three, following that by holing from 13 yards for another birdie at the fourth hole. Excitement was mounting as Charles dropped five shots behind.

By the turn, de Vicenzo, after an outward half of 33, was four behind Tony, while Charles and O'Connor were one shot further back. As the second nine progressed, all the challengers dropped out except Charles, who birdied the 10th and then the 13th, where Tony bogied the hole, leaving him with a three-shot lead until the 17th, where he three-putted.

As they stood on the 18th tee, Tony was two shots in front. A par at the last hole would give him a round of 72. It was Charles to drive.

'Bob hooked it slightly–for him to the right, a slice for me. I always wonder about gamesmanship and golf. It just happens that I always watch the result of the other guy's shot–I'm just curious I suppose. There's a trap on the right-hand side of that 18th hole and Bob's ball bumped down and went past the trap into the light rough. He picked up his tee, looked down the fairway and said to his caddie: "God, it's in the trap, I'm sure it's in." I never said anything. I knew bloody well it wasn't in. Whether his objective was to try to make me nervous of the trap–I don't know. I've never brought it up with him, I don't care to, it doesn't matter any more. But it didn't have any effect–I knew it wasn't in the trap.

'I said to myself you've got to make a good swing, hold on with your left hand, and as I was saying it, I was doing it. I looked up and saw the ball going right down the centre of the fairway. I walked after it and then Bob played his second from the rough, and he put it 20 feet from the pin.

'The shot I had left was one I had been practising all week. I had 140 yards to go, which is a very soft seven iron and I had been practising my rhythm and tempo all week with a seven iron. I managed to play it nicely to about 12 feet, after which I felt marvellous but not yet that I'd won.

'Then I was walking through the crowds swarming on the fairway. I lost my shoe, managed to retrieve it and went towards the green. I was thinking I might six putt–I didn't dare think I'd won, not until the last putt went in the bottom of the hole. It's not impossible to three putt in that situation and Bob could have single-putted and we would have tied.

'The crowd was going berserk and I couldn't really enjoy it, although I did in that I knew it was happening. But I didn't say, that's it, isn't it great. I'd seen enough to know that you never count your chickens. I said, you haven't done it yet, you have 12 feet to go.

'When Bob missed from 20 feet I felt better and he holed out for his par. Then two putts later it was all over.

'As I came off the 18th green, Jack Nicklaus was there, and he was one of the first guys to congratulate me. I said to him: "Jesus Christ, I never thought I could be that nervous and play golf." He laughed and replied, "I know. Isn't it great?" obviously realising the situation and knowing how it was. He was the one man in the whole of the British Isles at that time whom I knew would understand what I was saying–I couldn't have said it to anyone else. I'll never forget how I felt, and nor have I ever forgotten him saying that.

'I don't envy anyone in the world. But to be in a position to say, I know, isn't it great–and he meant it because he had experienced that situation so many times–then I envy him.

'After that I was numb for 24 hours. I was spent, elated. You win the Open Championship, but you don't go out, go up to someone and say, Hi, I'm Tony Jacklin, I won the Open yesterday. It's personal. It's something which is yours alone.'

4: Hazeltine

FOLLOWING HIS British Open win, Tony continued his pattern of playing in America and coming back to Britain for a few tournaments. Really, he would have preferred to play more at home, to savour his victory. He did nothing of note on the US tour for the rest of the year and he returned to come third in the Dunlop Masters in October. In 1969 he won $59,545 on the world money list, which put him in 33rd place.

At the beginning of 1970 he started well in America by tieing Pete Brown in the Andy Williams Open at San Diego, but he lost the play-off. When the tour moved to Florida, he was finishing consistently high: tied 8th at Doral, tied 4th at Monsanto, 3rd at Jacksonville, tied 11th at Greensboro, tied 12th in the Masters, 2nd in the Tournament of Champions.

When he played at home he won the Wills Open with rounds of 67, 65, 66, 69, which put him seven shots ahead of the rest of the field. Later in the year he won the Lancome Tournament in France with an eagle, birdie finish. His world money earnings that year were to jump to $144,106, putting him in sixth place.

Back in June, in America, the week before the US Open at Hazeltine, Minnesota, Tony missed the cut: 'I was not playing badly, but my putting was terrible. When we got to Hazeltine, Bert Yancey's brother, Jim, a professional, gave me a tip on the putting green to help me with my stroke. He said he found that you can regain feel if you stand over the ball, get ready to hit it, look at the hole and then hit the ball as you are still looking at the hole. It did give me a marvellous sense of feel through the ball, so I practised it–just on the putting green, not on the course–and it helped me to become very confident on the golf course with my putting.

'Hazeltine was not a very good golf course, but that was not my problem. My problem was playing it. It's a weakness to say any course is bad. When you're really playing well, you're on top of yourself and your game, you realise that all you've got to do is get the ball in the hole.

'Meanwhile, American professional Dave Hill, was making remarks– that Hazeltine should be ploughed up, that all it needed was 80 acres of corn and some cows–for which he was fined $150 by the American PGA.

'On the first day of the tournament it was very windy and everyone was having trouble. I thrived on it, enjoyed it, and took one shot at a time. Conditions were so difficult that you could not get ahead of yourself. My putting was super and it made a big difference when on the opening hole I got a birdie, by slotting in my first putt from 15 feet. After that they just kept going in. At the 17th–a short par four–I went in water and had a double bogey, but I still led by two shots, after a one under par 71.'

Watching Tony all that week at Hazeltine, was Ben Wright of the *Financial Times*, who was one of the three British journalists in attendance. 'The 1970 US Open was a highspot of my life,' says Ben. 'It was a hell of a thing. I had the feeling Tony was going to win from the first day, because absolutely nothing went wrong.

'The second hole of the tournament he hooked into the bushes, leaving himself a shot to the green that needed to be played through a hole about three feet square. He took a two iron and the shot came off. Every putt he looked at went in, and you got the idea that someone up there was with him that week, who had never been so with him before or since–there was an absolute inevitability about it from the first day onwards.

'Tony was totally bemused and more than a little scared each night. He, Viv and I, went out to eat Chinese food in the evenings in Minneapolis, and he was getting more tense each evening. He was slightly hysterical, giggling, at a high pitch of excitement. It all got a bit crazy one evening, just because he was so much on edge.

'I was excited beyond belief, absolutely like a dog with two tails. I was strutting about the place with my chest out. As no one British had done anything for so long, it was a rare moment for me.

'In the first round the wind was gusting at 40 mph and it was colder than you could believe–Minnesota at its worst–but a typical Scunthorpe November day, and Tony was absolutely in his element. It was a day for Guinness and fish and chips, and he reacted just as he should have done– got his head down and battled it out. Most of the great players who hit the ball too high, backed off–they were muttering and moaning, and a lot of players flung in the towel that first day.

'On the second day the weather was slightly better, and as the week went on it became sunny and hot for the last two days. Tony played the second round well, with a two under par 70, and he increased his lead to three shots ahead of the outspoken Dave Hill.

'He was on a cloud, he could do no wrong,' continues Ben. 'If he dropped a shot, he came back with a birdie putt. In the first two rounds he missed a lot of greens, but infallibly he got down in two shots, holing from four to six feet like clockwork, which is normally the weakness of his game.

'There is no question that in his whole career his weakness has been holing out. He's really been less than a world-class putter. But for one magical week at Hazeltine he was a world-class putter and I don't think he was before or has been since.'

In the third round Tony was paired with Dave Hill, who had become a controversial figure. 'He'd made himself a bad boy,' says Tony, 'and I felt he was taking a lot of the heat off me. I was going to let him do all the bloody talking, and I was going to do the playing.'

Says Ben Wright: 'Dave Hill tried very hard to unsettle Tony by niggling him and by nattering. Generally, he tried a little gamesmanship. The crowd hated Dave for what he had said about the golf course, and he was "mooed" all the way round. His remarks were totally justified, but he was the wrong man to make them.

'It was rather a bad golf course with nearly every hole a dog-leg, which seemed unnecessary as it was lovely rolling Minnesota farmland with acres of room. There were some good holes towards the end, but on the whole they lacked definition. That doesn't detract from Tony winning there – rather the reverse, as it wasn't easy and they all have to get it in the hole, which was very difficult.

'Tony was a gutsy player and justly famous for it. The American crowds at Hazeltine loved him. He was popular and they cheered him.'

Tony scored a further sub-par 70 in the third round, increasing his lead to four shots ahead of Dave Hill as he went into the final round.

'I went into the locker room that last day,' says Tony, 'where the Press were all asking me how I felt, what I'd eaten for breakfast and things like that. I opened my locker door and saw this sign saying "tempo" which I knew was from Tom Weiskopf and it was really nice.

'You can only feel so much pressure, so nervous in a tournament, then you have to think of having a job to do, of playing golf. It's difficult. I never indulge in thoughts of winning. If you're cheeky enough to do that beforehand, golf pulls the carpet from under your feet.

'I started the last round steadily and then lost it. At the seventh hole I hit a marvellous four iron over a water hazard to four feet, and missed it. Everything had been perfect until then and it was the first sign of danger of the whole week. At the eighth – a par three over water – I hit a two iron to the back of the green to about 30 feet from the hole, left the first putt five feet short, and missed that. I thought, oh shit.

'At the ninth, I pulled my tee shot by being a bit quick – panic was setting in. From the rough I got on the green with a four iron and was left with an uphill putt of about 30 feet. I hit it too bloody hard, it was going like a train but it hit the back of the hole, jumped up six inches into the air and dropped back in the cup.

'It was as though someone had lifted an anvil off my back. If that putt hadn't gone in, I wouldn't have won that tournament. Although you make your own luck on the golf course, and you have to be an optimist, things which happen like that putt turn tournaments and only you know.'

Someone else who knew was standing at the sidelines – Ben Wright: 'It was a dreadful putt – it could have gone 10 feet past the hole. I shut my eyes and thought he'd knocked it off the green. He was certainly edgy, it was a neurotic stab, but when it went you knew there was no problem.

'Tony went on to score three more birdies in the final holes. Towards the end I was communicating the scores of the other players to him. On the 15th, a USGA chap threw me off the course – from inside the ropes; he said it was not my business to be giving the latest information to Jacklin, and I was not to get near the players. I threatened to kill the guy I was so annoyed. After that I stayed outside the ropes and Tony came across.

Left: *The final putt at Hazeltine.* Right: *Back to school. Scunthorpe's most famous old boy returns to his seat of learning.*

'Tony's final birdie came in dramatic style on the last green, as he became the new US Open champion by holing out from 30 feet and winning from Dave Hill by a margin of seven shots.

'That last evening when we were celebrating, Tony was emotionally as high as a kite—an elation born of extraordinary success, almost hysteria, and particularly due to the enormity of the eventual winning margin.

'I got so drunk, I was screaming down the streets of Minneapolis in the early hours of the next morning. I was haywire. On the aeroplane home I was so hung over and drunk, that the stewardess had to give me oxygen as I was in danger of passing out. I flew home via Chicago, and happened, by chance, to get on the same flight as Tony and Vivien and we had more than a few drinks.

'It was something I'll never forget—definitely a highspot of my golfing existence. I'm not going to experience anything like that ever again because there won't be another British player winning the US Open probably in my lifetime. And if there is, it is going to be the first one that you always remember. It was such an extraordinary victory.'

Tony savoured his victory with Vivien, who had been following him all week, alternating with attending to seven-month-old Bradley, who was cutting his first tooth: 'We all shared one room,' says Viv, 'and Bradley would stand up and shake the cot with his teething. I spent half the week in the bathroom with him at nights, so that Tony could sleep undisturbed.'

The congratulations poured in, from the famous and the not so famous. From a George Tarbuck of Liverpool came one of the many thousand admiring letters:

Dear Mr Jacklin,

After the deflation of the World Cup, and the more recent anni-
hilation of England in the Test Match, it has been a simply
wonderful experience to see the Americans trailing after
England's No. 1 golfer. The other two events were team games,
but your achievement was, very simply, Tony Jacklin versus the
Rest of the World, and my goodness I could jump for joy in the
manner of your superb execution of all the big names in golf.

To crown your effort with that 'out of this world' putt on the
last green, when that 30 feet seemed half a mile to me, I nearly hit
the ceiling when I saw it go down. That shot should be shown on
the 'telly' every day until the next championship (and any other
time when the country gets a setback).

Thank you Tony for the pride you have brought back to Limey
Land and long may your driver and your putter put 'em down.

A gentleman called G. A. Wilson, of Wallasey, Cheshire, addressed his
highly ink-stained postcard to: Tony Jacklin, British Open Golf Champion, England, Great Britain (and the Post Office sensibly observed on
the card, try Scunthorpe, Lincs) and the text read:

Please accept my congratulations, I am delighted. Now relax and
fish. 50 years we have waited (not me I'm 47 years young). I'd love
to play 18 holes with you – no handicap.

From the late Bing Crosby, came a letter signed, Your friend, Bing:

Dear Tony:

Your thrilling victory is the greatest thing that's happened to
international golf in many years. That was a truly great performance. Warmest congratulations and best wishes for many
more important victories to come.

From racing driver Jackie Stewart and his wife Helen came a telegram:

Congratulations on a wonderful performance. What are you
going to do with all the money?

The messages of goodwill flowed in, including one sent by the Duke and
Duchess of Windsor from their ship at sea.

Tony's own reaction to his US Open victory was this: 'It gave me a hell
of a lot of satisfaction to do it. It was another feather in my cap. Knowing
what I know now, I'd rather have won another Open Championship, the
only one that means anything to me. But I'm glad I won the US Open and
showed them what I could do. It was like putting two fingers up to the
Americans and they can say what they like, but they can't all put their
names on the Cup.'

5: Star Treatment

WINNING THE Open Championship in 1969 made Tony a national hero. Adding the US Open title within a year gave him superstar status, and with it went the superstar treatment that is afforded to our heroes.

The awards, the recognition, the feting, came thick and fast. In 1969 he was *Daily Express* Sportsman of the Year–the award was presented by Harold Wilson. He received the British Golf Writers' Trophy and the American Metropolitan Sportswriters' award. The National Sporting Club honoured him with a dinner.

A waxwork of Tony went into Madame Tussaud's in London, and it stayed there until 1976 when it was moved to a paper mill owned by Tussauds, near Wells in Somerset, where it is still on display.

A bronze was made of Tony's head, which was purchased by a gentleman from Lincolnshire after it was exhibited at the Royal Academy in London. A coral-coloured Tony Jacklin rose was produced, that perhaps by any other name would not have smelt as sweet. Tony was entertained to lunch at 10 Downing Street, when Prime Minister Edward Heath was entertaining the President of Singapore, himself an ardent golfer.

In the 1969 BBC Sports Personality of the Year ballot, Tony was runner-up to Ann Jones, who won Wimbledon that year–the week before Tony won the Open Championship. The following year when Tony won the US Open, the award went to the boxer Henry Cooper for winning the European Heavyweight Championship: 'It doesn't make any difference what people think,' says Tony, 'but no one has ever seen a ballot and no one knows how it is done. I do know that more people in Britain watched that US Open win recorded on television, than Americans who were viewing it at the time. After winning the US Open I was disappointed again not to get the BBC Sports Personality award.

'After that, I said if ever I was fortunate enough to win, I would never go. I think the powers that be gave it to the sentimental favourite of the time because Henry was at the twilight of his career. I've nothing against Henry–he's one of the great guys of all time and a great pal of mine.'

One award that was accorded to Tony in 1970 was the Order of the British Empire. 'I felt good about that. I thought it was nice to get it. But when you are actually getting it, there are so many hundreds of people that it doesn't seem so special any more. I felt maybe I should be getting knighted–there weren't so many of them! The Queen said, "It's a pleasure to give you this, I've watched you on television," and she wished me luck.'

Further recognition came as Tony left Buckingham Palace that day and he found himself the subject of the television programme *This is Your Life* although he had nearly gone before they could catch him. Plans had been made through his wife, Vivien: 'I went with Tony and his mother to London for the presentation of the OBE. We stayed at the Savoy Hotel and I made sure that Tony had enough appointments to keep him busy and we could go to a rehearsal for *This is Your Life*.

'Eamonn Andrews told me to bring Tony out through the main gate of Buckingham Palace and he would be waiting there. When we came out, it was raining, and Tony, having got through all his appointments and finished the ceremony in the Palace, wanted to be home and he said, "come on we'll get a cab out the back." I told him we were being met with a car and managed to get him out the front, where Eamonn came up to him.

'He couldn't believe it. "No, not me," he said; he was about the first young person (he was 26) to be on the programme. They took him off and I didn't see him again until we were on stage. Bert Yancey was flown over from America; Jimmy Tarbuck was there, Bill Shankland from Potters Bar, his caddie Willie Hilton, and many others. It was a lovely gesture.'

About three years after his first visit to the Palace, Tony received another Royal summons: 'I was asked to lunch at the Palace, but I couldn't go because I was in America, so I wrote a letter explaining that. Then a couple of months later Vivien got a 'phone call from Lord Plunkett, asking me to go to lunch at the Palace. At first Viv thought it was Jimmy Tarbuck on the 'phone, but it was genuine and I was asked to be there at ten minutes to one, for one o'clock.

'I took a cab, went into the Palace and met this marvellous woman, Lady Hussey, who was Princess Margaret's Lady-in-Waiting. I thought straight away, what a nice person she was—really loose and easy to talk to. So within two minutes of being there, I said, what time do they get up in the morning? She said, "about eight. I suppose you think this is all marvellous, but it's just like anything else for us." I said I didn't think it was so marvellous and I wouldn't want to swop places. Then we chatted about my golf and travelling around, and I asked how many would be at the lunch, expecting a big affair. She said, "there are only seven of you."

'The Queen, Prince Philip, and Princess Margaret were all there. Before we had lunch, Princess Margaret took me out on the terrace, showed me the garden and we had a pleasant chat.

'We went into lunch and I remember the Chairman of ICI, an Orthopaedic Surgeon, a Journalist and a Silversmith were there. The Chairman of ICI sat between me and the Queen.

'It was just like having lunch at home. Everybody was loose as a goose—it was terrific. You sit there thinking, Jesus Christ, pinch me, I'm at Buckingham Palace and it's just like anywhere else. The waiters were coming and giving us whatever we needed, everyone was laughing and joking, it was very informal and nice.

'After lunch I got talking to the Queen about shooting and deer-stalking, because I had been up to the north of Scotland deer-stalking at one time. There was this fellow who was a gillie, called Jock and he was our stalker and a right bastard. I was telling the Queen how he almost killed us by walking us off our feet, and how a mate of mine, who was about 42, nearly had a heart attack.

'The Queen sympathised with me and said that gillies were usually very hardy . . . a race apart. I said, with the greatest respect, I don't think they are as hard at Balmoral as this fellow was with us. And she started to laugh – she enjoyed that and chuckled. She's more royal than the rest. She doesn't really indulge herself too much and you can't imagine her having a good belly laugh.

'The Duke was more jovial and informal than she was capable of being. He talked about golf and I told him he should play. He said he had hurt his wrist playing polo and it wouldn't stand up to it. I said, once you started to play, you wouldn't think there's any other game, I promise you. He said, "yes, well I've got a few holes in the garden at Windsor."

'I enjoyed meeting the Queen more than anyone I've ever met. I didn't feel in awe of her – I've never felt in awe of anyone. There are a lot of successful people around, but there's only one Queen of England and it's nice to meet her, and the Duke and the Royal Family. They've all got a tremendous job to do and they can't get out of it.

'Like Princess Margaret – she gets criticised tremendously and it's not bloody easy. She's always got to be there being the Princess. I don't feel sorry for them, but I do understand it.

'I enjoyed chatting to the Queen – a couple of minutes of a lifetime. It was interesting to have done that. She impressed me as very regal. I'm pleased I made her laugh – she's got a sense of humour but she doesn't overdo it.

'I'm sure it's refreshing for her to meet someone like me – I'm glad I could fit in. I bet she enjoyed having me there, more than some formal Emperor. We had a laugh and a joke, a nice lively chat.

'If I could choose to spend time with any member of the Royal Family there's absolutely no question that it would be Prince Charles. I don't hero worship anyone but I think he's fantastic. He manages to steer clear of bad publicity and usually gets a good Press. I know from King Constantine that he has a marvellous sense of humour, and you can tell that from reading about him. He does a marvellous job and carries it off in a totally professional manner. He's probably got the most personality of anyone in public life in Britain. He has great presence and individuality.

'I wouldn't want to meet him in a false situation. It would be marvellous if he took up golf. I was sorry he was away when I went to the Palace.

'I met Princess Anne about a month after I was at the Palace, at the *Daily Express* Sports Personality awards. We were chatting and she said, "Oh Mummy told me you were over for lunch the other day. I was sorry to miss you." Princess Anne took a lot of stick for a long time from the Press but she went ahead and did her own thing. I admire that.

Above: *The last Britons to win the Open Championship, Tony and Max Faulkner, play a Cancer Relief charity match with Henry Cooper and Eric Sykes.*

S.S. Michelangelo
At Sea.
As from - 4 Route du Champ d'entraînement
Paris.16ème
June 23, 1970.

Dear Tony Jacklin,

        Although we have never met I have been following your fortunes on the "Circuit" for the last few years.

        I was therefore thrilled as a compatriot and a keen golfer to learn from this ship's radio of your great 7 stroke win in the US Open at Chaska, Minnesota.

        Unfortunately The Duchess and I sailed June 19 from New York so that I was deprived of watching your last two rounds on T.V.

        I am therefore proud to congratulate you on this triumph and for being the first Britisher to win the U.S. Open since 1912. This feat plus your winning the British Open last year surely elevates you to the golfers' "Hall of Fame" alongside the other great champions who have preceded you.

        I hope we may meet some day. In the meantime I send you my best wishes for continued big victories in your golfing career.

        Sincerely Yours,

        Edward
        Duke of Windsor

Mr. Tony Jacklin
East Lodge
Elsham
Brigg - Lincolnshire
England.

Top: *The seating plan for Tony's lunch at Buckingham Palace.*

Centre: *The letter from the late Duke of Windsor.*

Left: *'I'll guard this Cup, you clean that one'. Tony with the Open Championship trophy, Viv with a replica of the US Open trophy.*

'I went shooting with her husband, Captain Mark Phillips in Norfolk. That's the way to spend time with people – informally.

'I took up shooting when I was about 14 and I shot anything that moved. Then I got friendly with the farming community in Norfolk and went shooting grouse and pheasant on the farms, or in Scotland. I'm not over the moon about the shooting aspect of it, but as a sport it's gone on for centuries and I suppose you can say man is a hunter. I enjoy it to a point, but it's not always the reason I do it. It's an opportunity to meet a different cross-section of people – the farmers and people of the land.'

Playing golf has brought Tony into contact with a host of famous names, and one member of Royalty whom he particularly liked was Ex-King Constantine of Greece: 'I have played golf with him twice. Once was in the pro–am before the Italian Open at Rome in 1973, which I won. He's a very nice guy and it was good fun.

'He asked me to invite a few friends to his house for dinner one night and I remember Jack Newton, Clive Clark, Peter and Anne Oosterhuis, and John Cook were among those who were there.

'I always remember this great punch bowl he had full of Beluga caviar and we were told to help ourselves with a punch ladle. We would go over and take a huge scoop of Beluga caviar – the contents must have cost £200 – and the then Shah of Iran had sent it to him the week before.

'I really liked him. He's a super guy with a great sense of humour. We got to telling jokes and as the evening went on the jokes got worse and worse. King Constantine said that he keeps in close touch with Prince Charles, and how he would love to have been there for the joke session.'

Another evening much enjoyed by Tony and his friends was one given by Walter Annenberg, who, in 1970, was American Ambassador in London. 'He invited me and some friends to dinner at the Ambassador's residence in Regent's Park, after I won the US Open, as a gesture on behalf of his country. I really liked him and felt he was a super chap. It came up in conversation that he likes the same poem that I have pinned up in my study, a bowdlerised version of Rudyard Kipling's *If*:

'If you think you're beaten you are
If you think you dare not you don't
If you'd like to win but you think you can't
It's almost a cert you won't
If you think you'll lose you've lost
For out in the world you'll find
Success begins in a fellow's will
It's all in the state of a mind
Life's battles don't always go
To the stronger or faster man
But sooner or later the man who wins
Is the man who thinks he can'

'Walter Annenberg was very interested in that, and it turned out that he had all sorts of sayings and he put some on paper and sent them to me. He's a very nice, tremendously wealthy man, who has his own golf course with his home at Palm Springs in California. It was a delightful evening in Regent's Park.'

Show business and professional golf have much in common and many of the great personalities in show business also have a feeling for golf and and the pro golfers. Many of them sponsor tournaments on the American Tour, including Bob Hope, the late Bing Crosby, Andy Williams, Jackie Gleason and Glen Campbell: 'I know them all,' says Tony. 'When you are successful you have an automatic "in" with other successful people.

'I feel I've more in common with successful people, but they can't live together very long because they all have egos that need feeding. In the south of Spain you may find Sean Connery, James Hunt, Jimmy Tarbuck and Tony Jacklin playing golf together for a few days. That's fine but then we split up and do our own thing, before we spoil it.

'Of course I've met all the Hollywood stars who play golf, such as the late Bing Crosby, Howard Keel, Dick Martin, Fred MacMurray, Robert Stack, Bob Hope, Dean Martin and Vic Damone. I've played golf with them, and I used to play in the Los Angeles Pro–Am with Andy Williams, whom I really like.

'I met Frank Sinatra in Biarritz on the west coast of France, when I was playing in an exhibition and he was staying at the same hotel. He came out and watched us and we found that my partner at the Bing Crosby used to be his Press agent. Sinatra was on holiday in Biarritz and he had his own DC9 in which he offered me a ride back to New York with him the next day. I couldn't go because I had to leave that night.

'I liked him very much. I love his records. He's a regular guy, loose, with a nice personality–I know other guys who know him and think the same. I understand how he feels persecuted by the Press and I feel sorry for him although it's part of the price you pay and everyone accepts that. Sinatra pops someone on the nose and there's going to be law suits from time to time, but his concerts are always a sell out.

'I think it's quite easy to be a top singer. It's not easy to get there, but it's a breeze to make a living that way. Sinatra's job is so much easier than Nicklaus's. All Sinatra does is get up and sing 'Come Fly With Me' and a bunch of those songs he made famous over a 30- to 40-year career– and everyone goes bananas. Nicklaus still has to win a tournament every week or he's finished. All Sinatra does is sing.

'These guys don't necessarily have the greatest voices in the world. There are a million guys in a million clubs who sing the same as they do. It's the star quality which counts and that is created by the Press who put his picture in glossy magazines and stir public emotions.

'Muhammad Ali's job is so much more difficult than Sinatra's it's a joke, and Ali's not as tough as Nicklaus. Ali's world champion and everyone says he's the greatest. When he has to fight he puts on his track suit every morning and grinds it out. Sinatra can do what he likes and as long as his tie is straight and his hair combed he's all right. He opens his mouth and the same noise comes out. Singers have it made.

'It's fun to meet the stars and you learn that they are just people, but you know they understand and maybe have the same problems as you do. You can't explain to someone what it's like to go into a room full of people when everyone starts talking and nudging each other – it's uncomfortable.

'I could go with Sean Connery to a pub, when I wouldn't go in on my own – he'd probably belt them if there were any trouble. I don't feel comfortable, like one of the lads in a pub, and that's what I really like to be. I like jokes – telling them and listening to them. I don't particularly like the beer, I like the company.

'But someone points you out, asks for an autograph, makes you feel uncomfortable. I try not to subject myself to it. I stopped going to pubs years ago. I'm not complaining about it, I realise it's something I can't do any more. Maybe when I'm 55 or 60, I'll be able to go in a pub, get all the cronies round and tell them all the old stories.

'At first it's nice being famous – part of you likes it, the ego part. It's nice when you go in a restaurant and get a bloody good table. You want to make people sit up and probably if it didn't happen you would wish people did ask for your autograph. I was very sensitive at first and wanted everyone to like me. I never did anyone a bad turn, I went about my job the best way I could and didn't talk down to anyone. But even when you go out of your way to be nice, someone will think you're a pain in the arse. Some people make a hobby of picking others to pieces.

'I remember being at the Marine Hotel at Troon one year and I'd been playing with Tom Weiskopf, Jack Nicklaus and Lanny Wadkins. I was walking through the lobby to the dining room and a guy stopped me and said, "how is it I used to like you when you started out and now I think you're a big head?" He'd had a few drinks. I replied, well you're entitled to your opinion, that's all right, I'm sorry but what can I tell you? Then I said excuse me, went to get by, and he said, "there's no need to be off-hand." I said, what do you expect me to say, something nice? Then I told him to piss off. Tom Weiskopf was hovering around behind me because he thought I might be in a bit of trouble.

'It upset me that night – the fact that someone would go out of their way to come up and say something unpleasant. There are so many crazy people.

'Now if a guy comes up to me and says I don't like you – I say, great. It doesn't bother me any more. I walk through a room without looking at anyone so that I don't have to get involved. I hate cocktail parties and all the same polite chit-chat. I like to be myself and I love to talk to people on their own. I may be over-reacting but I'm entitled to live my life as anyone else is – the way I want to live it. I really am.'

6: Open Wounds

AFTER WINNING the 1970 US Open at Hazeltine, Tony was on a high. His next major event was the Open Championship at St Andrews, where he was defending his title.

By now, Tony was a household name, an international star, shining bright. He was also heavily involved with all sorts of promotions and commitments, which kept him on a hectic schedule round the world, and which gave rise to plenty of criticism that he was too far stretched to be able to give of his best on the golf course.

The first round of his defence at St Andrews began in amazing fashion: 'I played magical golf. The putts started going in–it was as though I had a hot-line to the hole. On the first three holes I drew back the putter and those three putts, two from 15 feet and one from five feet, went straight into the hole and I was three under after three holes.

'I had a par at the 4th, birdied the 564-yard 5th, where I was on in two and had two putts; I just missed a birdie at the 6th, birdied the 7th from six feet, and had a par at the 8th. At the 9th, I hit a one iron off the tee, pulled it slightly into the rough, and had just over 100 yards to the flag. I took a wedge, and the ball bounced slightly short of the flag, then hit it and dropped right into the hole. I was out in 29 and seven under par for the first nine holes.

'I went eight under as I birdied the 10th from six feet. I just missed chances to birdie the 11th and 12th, and had a par at the 13th. I drove well at the 14th, then, as I swung the club back on my second shot, I heard someone in the crowd shout out "fore"–I don't know why but my concentration wavered and I heaved off the ball and hit it into a gorse bush.

'It had been terribly sultry and quiet, and the sky was looking really threatening. Suddenly, there was thunder and great flashes of lightning, and by the time I reached my ball, after my second shot on the 14th–the course was under water. The greens were unplayable and there was no question of going on, it was a freak storm.

'It was a significant moment when you consider that finally I missed a putt of 10 feet on the 72nd hole and came fifth–if I'd made it I would have tied Lee Trevino and Harold Henning in third place. I was on 286, three shots behind Nicklaus and Sanders.

'I had to go back at 7.30 am the next day to finish my round. I had to drop out of the bush and on the 14th and I made six on that hole. I dropped two more shots on the last four holes, but whereas the day before it had been a drive and pitch to the 15th and 16th, and it had been possible to drive the 18th, now it needed a four and five iron for the second shots, and it was impossible to hit the 18th with a driver. I finished with 67, which was disappointing when something like a 62 had seemed possible.

'I continued with ever-increasing scores in the Championship, taking 70 in the second round that same day; then 73 in the third round to tie me with Nicklaus and Sanders, two strokes behind the leader, Lee Trevino.

'I was in with a chance on the last day, until I bogied the 16th by three putting, then found myself in loose stones near the Road at the 17th and took five on that hole. I finished in 76, with a par at the last hole, and it was just not good enough.

'It was awful to have your momentum going as I did on that first day, and then not be able to finish your round. People say the whole round should have been wiped out and that I was lucky. Many people think that because it was me we were brought back the next day, when in fact it is the tournament ruling.

'Obviously if I could have finished that day, even in 65 . . . but there I'm dreaming – it's all castles in the air.'

That Open Championship ended not only in disappointment for Tony, but with Doug Sanders becoming a tragic figure, missing his short putt to win on the 72nd hole, followed by the anti-climax of a play-off and victory for Jack Nicklaus.

The following year Tony's schedule was no less hectic, and in June he defended his US Open title at Merion but missed the half-way cut.

He went to the Open Championship in July at Royal Birkdale, where he put up a strong challenge to finish third, two shots behind winner, Lee Trevino, who had just won the US and Canadian Opens, and one shot behind the smiling, hat-doffing Liang Huan Lu from Formosa.

Tony had been fighting a hook all week, and after the third round he was tied with 'Mr Lu' just one shot behind Trevino. Pulling his shots the last day, Tony dropped three shots in the first nine holes, but managed a birdie spurt on the inward half that gave him a creditable round of 71, a total of 280, but not quite good enough to win.

Tony's record in the Open Championship since 1967 now showed: 5th in 1967 at Hoylake, tied 18th in 1968 at Carnoustie, 1st at Royal Lytham, 5th at St Andrews and 3rd at Royal Birkdale. It was a tremendous effort.

The 1972 Open Championship at Muirfield was to prove one of the most devastating moments of Tony's life, and of his golf career. The 1970 and 1971 Open Championships had been major disappointments in not providing Tony with another victory, but they paled in comparison to the shattering experience of 1972.

Earlier in the year Tony had achieved a further milestone in his career by winning a second Jacksonville Open, showing the talent was still there, giving his status in golfing terms another boost and doing wonders for his natural self-confidence. He knew he still had it in him to make the effort for the big occasion, to stand up to the pressure of another Open win, and at Muirfield the scene was set for what so nearly became his second Open win. But in reality it turned out to be a nightmare and a turning point for Tony, which to a great extent undermined that wonderful self-confidence. 'Nothing really good ever seemed to happen after Muirfield,' he claimed.

Tony's constant source of worry with his golf was his putting. He began the first hole of the Open Championship at Muirfield by three-putting for a bogey and ended the round in similar fashion, as he charged a 30-foot putt at the 18th for his birdie, went four feet past, and missed the return. But he played some great golf between the first and 18th, reflected by the five birdies in his round of 69, where he holed some very good putts which prompted him to comment, seemingly forgetting Jacksonville: 'They were the sort of putts I haven't been holing this year, and the sort a winner must hole.'

Tony's opening round in the Championship put him one shot behind Yorkshireman Peter Tupling, one ahead of Jack Nicklaus, and two ahead of Lee Trevino.

After a second round of 72 Tony shared the lead at the end of the day with Lee Trevino who had scored 71, 70, for his 141 total. It had been a scorching hot day at Muirfield but only one person had broken 70, and that was Johnny Miller whose five under par 66 set a new course record and put him one shot behind the leaders. Jack Nicklaus said he had not played well for his 72, and he was tied two shots behind the leaders.

On the third day Tony was paired with Lee Trevino and they were last out in the field. Tony was three under par at the turn, having holed some magnificent long putts to keep abreast of Trevino who was slotting them in from all over the greens.

At the short 13th Tony hit his ball into the bunker on the left of the green. He left it in the sand with his next shot, then hit it out into the bunker across the other side of the green; he got that out and finally two-putted for a three over par six. 'In the third round of the God-damned tournament, I'm in contention and I take a triple bogey and you know what that's going to do to anybody. Well, I was fantastic–I really was. I'm not talking about what anyone else thinks, that's from my own point of view. I can remember saying to myself, somehow you're not going to let that worry you, it's nothing. It was a six on one hole, but it's finished and it's not going to help worrying. I had a great attitude towards it. I can say I was fantastic because I know how I've been since, in letting things affect me.

'I went on to the next hole. Trevino birdied the 14th and I birdied; he birdied the 15th and I birdied; he birdied the 16th, thinned the ball out of the trap, where it hit the bottom of the flag and went in the hole, and I parred. We both birdied the 17th–Trevino nearly eagled the hole. At the 18th we were both five under par. Trevino hit a fantastic drive straight down the middle and put a five iron through the green. I drove into the

50

left rough, then took a six iron and hit it on the front of the long green. It was me to putt as I was further from the hole. But it's a dumb thing to do in professional golf, to let the other player off the green play first, usually you offer him the option, but on this occasion Trevino said, "I'll come up" and I agreed. Then he chipped the damned thing in the hole again for another birdie. By now I was wishing I hadn't let him play – but the guy had asked and you don't like to refuse. I putted up to six feet and made it for a four, and it really was a big putt to make.

'So he finished with five successive birdies for a 66, holing two wedge shots and I think I'd done pretty damned well to stay with him for my 67, especially after my six on the par three. You can only do so much and I really did a good job there that day – I hung right in and felt good about it, and I'm saying to myself, patience lad – your time will come.

'We were out together again the next day and I was one shot behind Trevino who was on 207. It was the most fantastic Open – with Nicklaus six shots behind me, seven behind Trevino, and he was going for the Grand Slam having already won the Masters and the US Open that year. On the first tee Trevino said to me, "Well, Nicklaus might catch one of us but he ain't going to catch us both." When we were playing the 9th and Nicklaus stood on the 11th, he had passed us both.

'We both eagled the 9th where we were on the green in two. Trevino holed from 35 feet and I followed him in from 20 feet. There were two tremendous roars, and the film of the 1972 Open shows Nicklaus on the 11th tee backing off for Trevino's roar, then for mine. I continued to play very well, concentrating hard, and when we reached the tee at the par five 17th – we were both six under and needing level par to beat Nicklaus, who had finished with a 66, putting him on 279, five under par for the Championship.

'Trevino hooked his drive off the 17th tee into a bunker. I hit a perfect drive and then put my second just short of the green with a three wood. Meanwhile Trevino had played sideways out of the bunker, hit his third into the left rough, his fourth over the green, and he had given up.

'It was then my turn to play from a good position in the short rough on the left in front of the green. When I hit it, I thought it was a good chip. I know that some long time after, Tom Weiskopf was being questioned about dumb shots in golf, and he said that that chip was one of the dumbest shots he had ever seen. I was mad about that and I never said anything to him, but I thought how little he knew, and that he had never asked me about it.

'The course was very dry at that stage after a week of good weather and the green looked very hard, very fast and very brown. I had a lot of green to go over before I got to the hole, as the pin was tucked in near the back on the right. I played a chip and run with a pitching wedge, and honest to God I thought it was good, I truly did. I expected it to run forwards but instead it slowed down quickly and stopped about 16 feet short. I wasn't too worried, however, as Trevino had played four and was through the back of the green.

'Then he simply took a club out of the bag, never lined it up – took one look and hit the chip just like you would when you want to get the job over. And incredibly it went into the hole.

'My immediate reaction after all the events of the day before was that he'd had all the breaks up to that point but I thought it could be my turn next. When he chipped in, I reacted by thinking I'm not going to let him beat me that way, I'll hole this and still go to the 18th one up. So I gave my ball a bit of a dunk and it went two and a half feet past. I wasn't worried by the one coming back, but I just got quick on the putt through lack of concentration – though really the circumstances were more to do with it than anything – and I missed it. Once I'd three-putted he played the last hole perfectly, while I hit my second shot in the right-hand bunker and took five. The wind had gone out of my sails by then.

'It was one of those incredible situations that happen in life and one hopes that one is always on the doing and not the receiving end. I'm sure if you play long enough most everything can happen to you. But by ten-fold that was the worst shock I've ever had on the golf course. It was such an important event, it was in the one tournament that means more to me than any other in the world, and the only saving factor was that I'd already won an Open. If I'd never won one, then it would have been even worse.

'I went into a state of shock and it definitely took me a long time to get over it, if I ever got over it. I was just numb. I didn't weep or cry, knowing that nothing was ever going to change it, knowing that when I awoke the next morning it was still going to be the same. It took a week to realise it, and it was certainly the biggest shock I ever had. Losing that Open to Trevino was like Muhammad Ali must have felt when Henry Cooper knocked him on his arse.'

At the time in 1972, Trevino admitted that he was not giving the chip he holed at the 17th his full concentration. It was, for Jacklin, he said, 'the straw that broke the camel's back.' Now, Trevino looking back, comments: 'What a lot of people don't realise is that Tony didn't finish second to me at Muirfield, he finished third and I beat Nicklaus. When I chipped in at the 17th I was aiming at the hole – when you putt and chip, that's exactly what you aim at. If you're saying was I mad when I got over the chip, yes, I was upset at having hit the ball over the green, but you are still trying to hole it. Maybe my chipping in the ball did deflate Tony, but then he bogied the last hole. It's happened to me and I know how he feels about it. But there has to be a winner and there has to be somebody who finishes second. It just happened that I won, that's all.'

For Tony it was obviously not something he could take in his stride. To put so much store by one championship increases the tension to pressure-cooker level. He had given out so much in time, energy, motivation and

52

The final act in the 1972 Open Championship at Muirfield. Tony and Lee Trevino on the last green.

The high before the low:
Tony holes a putt in the
final round of the Open in
1972.

achievement; the effort and the strain over the years must have been enormous, and when it looked like the reward was there once again the shock of having it snatched from your very grasp must mean that you begin to experience feelings of self-doubt.

'It was the most significant thing that happened in my career and it sure as hell had a big effect. Anything after that may be insignificant, it was a crazy, incredible thing. Anyone who plays sport knows that it can happen, and when I came off the last green Arnold Palmer was there and said to me, "whatever you do, try not to let it affect the way you think." I knew what had happened to him in the 1966 US Open when he lost seven shots to Casper in the last nine holes, tied, and then lost the play-off. And I think that affected him because he only won odd tournaments after that. Some people can play a whole career and not have that happen to them in a major championship.

'You can say, that's the way it is, you've never won until the last ball is in the hole. But I felt bloody sick. Everyone had talked to me about the law of averages but they don't exist–that confirmed it, there's no such thing. Nothing's fair. Life and golf are for the takers, you've got to take it, grab it and keep it. Never give anything away, it's for taking–there's no question in my mind about that. It may be a hard outlook but life is that hard. There's no room for sentiment while you're doing it. You can like a person but it's very important to have a straightforward outlook because it is dog eat dog whether it's Nicklaus or whoever you're playing against. Nicklaus wants to win so badly and he wants it for himself.

'Of course it can be a matter of who does what and when, but I've never felt a lucky player over the years. I've never won anything without winning it–no one has ever missed a putt on the last green to let me win. If you miss a putt on the last green it's talked about for ever more, if it's the first no one remembers. Doug Sanders will never be forgotten for the putt he missed in the 1970 Open at St Andrews at the 18th, yet in his own heart maybe he thinks about another shot that cost him it more, but he's left looking foolish on the last hole. People play on that sort of thing and you start to believe it–like Oosty (Peter Oosterhuis) believes he's going to flash one to the right under pressure–he's read about it so often and done it so many times, that in the end he expects to do it.

'Until you've won a major championship you don't realise what it means, that the majors are really the only ones that matter. For a British player there's no greater tournament to win than the Open Championship for making money–and that's my profession. I was lucky to win the Open as a young British player with everything going for me. No one could have made more money out of winning one single tournament than I did out of winning that one.

'With the Open being played on links courses and thus having the factor of the inconsistent bounce, the player who wins is the player who can accept adversity the best–which is what I feel I did that week at

Left: *Tony resumes his interrupted first round at St Andrews in the 1970 Open Championship by dropping out of a bush on the 14th hole.* Right: *The last straw: Lee Trevino wins after chipping in at the 71st hole of the 1972 Open Championship at Muirfield.*

Muirfield. When I said to myself, you've made six let's get some birdies now, when you don't let little things or big ones affect you, realising and putting yourself above them, that's what it's all about.

'There are not many players around who are capable of doing that. There are players who are capable of winning golf tournaments, but very few who can do it when it matters. There always have been very few. Even now in the last 15 years there have only been a handful – and it has nothing at all to do with hitting a golf ball. It's purely and simply an attitude of mind. I think I react well to a crowd. It was always the case in the Open where the crowd would turn me on. I used to expect to hole a long putt because I would anticipate it through the crowd. I didn't have to work at getting up, I was up.

'Motivation and circumstances are crazy things. Winning can be as simple as a putt going in at the right time, or a chip, and thinking, I needed that. Inwardly you always know if it's a lost cause or not – you're honed in to the happenings. When you're on that level, when you know you're going to win, it's like corridors and lots of people banging into each other below you, and the higher the level you reach the more you concentrate and the better you are in control of yourself.

'It's like flying at 45,000 feet where there are no other 'planes and there's nothing to stop you. It's just a question of making your destination. You're not dodging around.'

7: The Aftermath of Muirfield

AFTER HIS BITTER defeat in the Open Championship at Muirfield, Tony stayed home to play golf in Europe. Understandably, his reaction was to miss the cut in the next tournament he played, the Benson and Hedges at Fulford Golf Club.

The following week at Wentworth, in the Viyella PGA Championship, he made one of his well-known charges. At the half-way stage he was nine shots behind the leader, John Garner, but with two great rounds of 68 he won the title by three shots from Peter Oosterhuis.

As the weeks of competition went on, Tony was an unbeaten member of the English team that won the Double Diamond event; he tied 5th in the Wills Open, came 4th in the John Player Classic, 2nd in the Dunlop Masters, and then as the season came to a close, he found himself once more in confrontation with Lee Trevino.

It was in the Piccadilly World Match-Play at Wentworth. Tony had beaten Grier Jones by 7 and 6 in the first round, while Trevino had beaten Doug Sanders 2 and 1. Trevino and Jacklin met in the semi-final.

After their morning 18 holes, Jacklin was four down to Trevino. In the afternoon Jacklin was inspired, and in the first nine holes he had an eagle, five birdies and three pars, to be out in a seven under par 29, and he was one up on Trevino.

At the short 10th, Trevino birdied from three feet to square the match. Jacklin holed from 14 feet to birdie the 11th and go one up. Trevino then eagled the long 12th to draw back to level. The next five holes were halved.

On the last hole, Jacklin's second shot went left of the green and he was 30 yards from the pin. Trevino then played a marvellous three wood to eight feet. Jacklin chipped up to seven feet, and Trevino putted, but his ball stopped just short of the hole. Jacklin just failed to hole his seven-footer, so in spite of a magnificent afternoon round of 63, he lost the match.

In the morning, before the match began, Tony had been slightly worried that Trevino's constant chatter on the golf course might prove distracting, and he had informed the Mexican that he didn't want to talk. 'Don't talk, just listen,' Lee retaliated.

'He always has an answer for everything,' says Tony. 'But Lee doesn't use gamesmanship, it's just letting off steam – it's nerves on his part and he can't help himself. It's no good trying to match him or combat it, you have to retain your own personality. He's fortunate that he's been able to use it to his advantage most of his career. We've had some great games and I've got the utmost respect for him – he's a great player.

'Losing to Trevino in the Match-Play was my own fault. I shot 63, but I missed the last green with my three wood and that was the shot which cost me the match. I was so sure I was going to beat him, but I let him win on that last hole.'

So Tony's year–the one that was the turning point in his life–ended with his world money winnings totalling $111,847. He had won a US tournament at Jacksonville and come 32nd on their money list. In Britain he won the Viyella PGA Championship, and £16,225, which put him just behind the leader, Peter Oosterhuis, who won £18,525.

In his personal life he had moved from Lincolnshire to his mansion in Gloucestershire, and just four weeks before the move, his second son, Warren, was born in September.

For the next two years, Tony concentrated on playing golf in Europe. He lost his player's card in America through not playing 15 tournaments, and instead he supported the home tour. He was successful in 1973 in Europe to the tune of nearly £25,000, winning the Italian Open and the Dunlop Masters title by seven shots. In 1974, he won the Scandinavian Enterprises Open by 11 shots, and £20,000 in prize-money.

In 1975 Tony gave up his Gloucestershire home and became a tax exile from Britain, in order to establish residency in Jersey. From April, he spent a disastrous few months with the whole family, including his new daughter, Tina, who was born in March, on the American Tour where he was given back his card.

'It was terrible, I was doing what other people thought I should do. I suffered the derogatory things the guys on tour were saying when I got back my player's card. I was grinding away, playing like a berk.

'One day when we were in Dallas, Jack Nicklaus gave me a ride in his car, and he asked me how I was playing. I said, not great. He replied, "you're having a tough time. If it's any consolation, I went through a similar period when I was about your age (30) and maybe it wasn't as bad as yours, but for me it was. I wondered whether I cared. I was very unsure, but I just wanted you to know that I came through it."

'I remember when Jack had problems with his game–it was prior to the 1970 Open at St Andrews. I played with him there in the last round and after we had finished playing we were standing watching Doug Sanders on the 18th green. Jack thought it was all over, but I said, I'd like to give you £10,000 for your chances right now.

'When Doug missed the putt, I've never seen such an amazing reaction from Jack because he suddenly realised that perhaps he could now win the title. And it was the same when he won the play-off against Doug Sanders and flung his putter into the air almost without knowing it–he was overjoyed because he had broken that bad spell.

'He must have felt under tremendous pressure at the time, having such high standards, having done so much and wondering whether he could keep it going. He came to terms with it and he came through it.

'I try to watch guys like that–he's a picture of determination and concentration, nothing else. He's business-like on the golf course, marching forwards.

'By that time, I had realised that no one could do better than Jack Nicklaus, and, to a point, it affected me. The great thing Jack had, was that he was doing it for reasons other than money. He has momentum going for him all the time.

'I get the feeling that no one will ever achieve in my lifetime what Nicklaus has done. I would bet £50,000 on it. So few people really know how fantastic he is.'

Tony's year of exile ended. He had won $10,824 in America and was in 123rd place. But his dilemma continued. He had changed his home, he was now rocketing between two tours, he was changing his golf clubs. A depression was beginning to set in, that he could not shake off.

'I was worrying about everything–people with cameras would bother me, or a kid moving behind the tee. I ended up a wreck. You've no idea how bloody low I got, wondering what was going to happen. I knew I had so much talent inside, but I would freeze and not let it come out. I couldn't swing I was trying so hard.

'I would play with fellows every week who couldn't play, but they shot 67 and I shot 72. It's a terrible thing to get in a frame of mind where you can't let it all happen because you're depressed and so nothing happens.

'It got really bad at the 1976 Bob Hope Desert Classic at Palm Springs. I had never been as nervous in my life playing golf as I was at the beginning of that tournament. I mean nervous, I'm not talking about keyed up. After playing a round I was in such a state that I had to go back and lock myself in my room for a couple of hours, and I would pass out on the bed. I was a gibbering wreck through anxiety, which is frightening.

'Then an American professional, George Burns said to me, "I've got this book *The Inner Game*, why don't you read it? It's about tennis, but you can apply it to golf–it concerns Mind One and Mind Two–the Ego Mind and the Subconscious Mind."

'I read the book and thought, you're going to make a swing and it's none of your business where the ball goes–just aim and release it. I was applying the theories of the book. In the last round at Palm Springs I made a bogey and a double bogey, I didn't putt well, but I still finished with a 67 to come joint 11th, which was my best placing of the year.'

At the end of 1976, Tony had won $18,000 on the US Tour. In Europe his winnings totalled £11,204 and he had won the Kerrygold International in Ireland, amid controversy, as he was put off first on the last morning, in spite of being a leader, in order to enable him to fly straight to America in time for the US Open.

His state of mind did not improve: 'Normally, you only get so nervous at a tournament and you control it but to be nervous and out of control as I was, that's the end of the world–there's no future in it.

Salt in the wound: Tony recovered from 4 down against Lee Trevino to take the lead, but lost on the 36th hole in the 1972 Piccadilly World Match-Play.

'It would eat my heart out when I read articles saying, he doesn't need the money, he doesn't want it, he's had the soft life too long, he doesn't care any more. If only they knew the nights I lay awake eating my heart out because I wasn't producing the results I had previously.

'Sometimes I would take Valium to help me sleep, because I was starting to have sleepless nights. If I had a big day ahead, I would take a pill at night to make sure I got the proper amount of rest. I was very conscious of the fact that I needed a lot of sleep at the time, and it seemed the logical thing to do. Now, I can survive on far less sleep, and I might take a couple of drinks in the evening to relax me.

'You can't take pills or drink to the extent that you're not aware of what you're doing. Once you lean on anything too much, it's a problem. I don't think I ever got to that stage. You need to be aware of reality – drink and pills dull the senses, and if you think they will change the way life is, you're an idiot.

'I can't be hypnotised – there's no way I would allow myself to be. Before the Uniroyal tournament at Moor Park in June 1977, I went to see a doctor in London because I was desperate about my state of mind – he tried to hypnotise me.

'He sat me in a chair, told me to shut my eyes, relax, and imagine I was doing something nice that I enjoyed. He said, "it's a lovely day, you're cutting the grass in straight lines, your wife has got a nice cold lager waiting for you" – but none of it worked.

'I did finish joint third in the Uniroyal, but there was no enjoyment in it for me whatsoever. Instead of thinking, my God, that was great, I might win next week – all I could think was, Christ, I've got to go and do this again next week. I thought how hard it was and I just didn't want to do it.

'I was living my life like that and it was bloody terrible. I never want to get like it again. You could kill yourself doing it like that–that's how people get to the point of jumping off buildings and you can understand it when everything gets right out of proportion.

'It got to the point where I knew I didn't want to be there, I was afraid to be around–it was awful. You don't want anyone to pull for you, you just want to disappear and for everyone else to disappear with you.

'People said that I didn't practise enough but my attitude is that I hit hundreds of thousands of golf balls when I was younger and I developed a swing that is the same most of the time, because I learned it long ago.

'Through the times I haven't been playing well, the problems have been in my putting and short game, not in my technique. I knew it would be a waste of time to hit balls on the practice ground in order to cure my putting problems.

'Although I was in an awful state of anxiety, I would never let myself get to where I gave up on everything, I wouldn't let that happen to me. My depression was confined to my golf–I didn't go home and beat my kids, or not talk to my wife.'

His wife, Vivien, coped as best she could with Tony's state of mind: 'I became part of it myself, watching Tony on the golf course, so I wasn't feeling on top of the world either. When you see what's happening, it's easier to understand and cope. But it is depressing to see it, and obviously I don't want to see Tony play badly.

'I've often walked round a golf course and wanted to scream or cry, but that's part of loving someone and having a husband.

'Sometimes the comments on the course were upsetting–like, he's useless, he's choking–and I would try to shut myself off from them, but I might let them affect me and come off the course feeling quite uptight.

'Tony got excited and tense when he was playing, and he knew that he felt anxious because he had not won for a long time. He would come home and we would discuss it and try to help each other, but there was not much I could do, except talk about why it might happen.

'I think you unwind by talking, but it's difficult to understand what's happening, because it's not a technical thing. I haven't any insight on it, as I haven't gone through it myself, and when it comes down to it I'm not the one who actually does it. But you're part of a person, and it is your business.

'I never felt it was anything to do with me–in that I hadn't caused Tony's anxiety on the golf course. He's never gone out and had to think about anything I've done.

'I'm pretty easy going, though I get wound up at times. I hide my feelings–I've learned to bottle them up, cope with them. You're so close to it all, there are so many ups and downs, and you just accept them.'

8: The American Influence

AMERICA WAS the making of Tony Jacklin. It was also his downfall. It became the story of when it was good it was very very good, and when it was bad it was terrible. He won the Open Championship because he had played in America. He succeeded over there through his guts, determination, ambition and talent. He failed there when he lost his way, when he didn't know what he was doing or why he was going.

After winning the two Opens, Tony was faced with a dilemma. He could grind it out on the US Tour, or be paid to play on a financially expanding European Tour, which greatly needed his presence for a selling point and for its further development. He came home in 1973 and the building up of the European Tour owed as much to him as the American Tour did to Arnold Palmer.

It proved an unsettling decision for Tony. His momentum in terms of the big occasion was probably at a low ebb, after the huge effort of the previous five years. Now he was faced with a Press and public expecting him to win every time he teed up the ball. This was obviously unlikely to happen, from an inspirational rather than a consistent player.

The level of competition and America had pulled it out of him before, where the constant pressure is tiring but keeps your mind sharp and your game at a high peak of performance. Jack Nicklaus can manage to raise his game at will, which is extraordinary. At least it's understandable for an American, playing primarily in his own country, having been bred on the American system of being madly competitive from birth and where it's of primary importance to win. Tony comes from a country of good losers, where the game's the thing.

When Tony lost his direction after 1972, he lost that positive attitude on the golf course. If you begin to wonder what you're doing and whether you're in the right place, you are questioning your desire and ambition.

Jack Nicklaus never did that. When he reached the position of needing a new goal, he made up his mind to win as many major titles as possible and to gear his life to doing just that. It was an attainable goal for him, and a limitless one. Also three out of four of golf's major championships are played in his own country. But Tony did not make the majors his aim. In fact, the problem was that eventually he did not have any aim at all.

Even though later it became a love-hate relationship, his American experience had not started in an unenthusiastic manner: 'When I was young, I identified with Elvis Presley. I liked the way he sang and tried to sing like him in the bath. I didn't make him a hero because I didn't have any heroes. I would not have asked him for his autograph–I've never in my life asked anyone for an autograph.

'But Elvis Presley being such a huge success made you feel that anyone who wanted to be that great had to go there, to the land of opportunity as that's where they catered for the stars. You see all the sparkling suits and the glory, but it takes time to find out that behind it there is an emptiness, which over the years became more difficult for me to accept.

'America gets written up as the be all and end all of everything. The vast sums of money the players are winning all the time whereby if you compare their top money winner with ours, it makes ours look like a pauper. Their country happens to be much wealthier, much younger, has more people and bigger prizes. The Americans are great at boosting their own egos–they are not necessarily that much better, but they tell themselves they are, whereas all we do is knock ourselves on the head, or we're prepared to give way and take second place.

'I don't rate that attitude. You're as good as anyone else if you think you are. The Beatles were the best, so was Tom Jones. Being British didn't hold them back–they had a belief in themselves.

'When I first went to America with Vivien in 1968, my ambition had no limits. It was marvellous, fantastic, and we enjoyed the hell out of it. I was as happy as Larry and wanted to be there more than any place in the world. The most terrific thing was when you hit a shot on the golf course, everyone went ooh! great, and it was conducive to your making good shots because you were rewarded for them.

'I had no family with me, I had a wife who was a partner, a girl friend really, somebody who was pulling for me just as much as I was, and we were going around everywhere together. It was great and there were no pressures to be back home.

'In latter years, as soon as I landed in America on my own, I thought, gee what am I doing here? Well, you've come to play golf so get on with it. You play for a week, call home every day and it becomes ridiculous. I did what I thought was right at the time, but in retrospect I think I was wrong to keep going back to America, because I'm British and for better or worse, this is where I belong.

'I know it used to annoy people when, after spending six months over there, I would come back with an American accent and I would get criticised for it. But when I'm anywhere for that length of time, something rubs off. I didn't have a public school education like Oosty, I went to Doncaster Road Secondary Modern in Scunthorpe. I'm also a great mimic, and if I weren't I wouldn't have been as good a golfer, because I copied anyone better than I was. If I talk to an Italian I speak to him in broken English; if I talk to Jewish people I shrug my shoulders. I know what I'm like and the last thing I need is for some idiot to tell me that I'm talking American. I know I'm doing it and I don't make any apologies for it.

'When I was in America I didn't really have a big following–it was all

Press talk. Palmer, Nicklaus and Trevino had a big following, but I was an impostor, a visitor, and I never established myself over there.

'Apart from the American champions, there were very few players who were not envious or jealous in some form or another, resenting my success. You can tell by the way a guy says well done—the one that means it and the one who says it because he feels he should, or the one who has to think before he says good shot. I would really have to think *not* to say good shot if someone does something good. But when you make a putt that matters—you know and they know—and there are those who clamp up and say nothing.

'Without any question I was accepted by champions like Nicklaus, Palmer, Trevino, Miller and Watson, because they were above any form of jealousy. They were all too involved in themselves which is right.

'Jack is above petty thoughts. He would always say good shot, whenever or wherever it was—the first or last hole. Arnold is not quite like that. He's so much for Arnold he can't see anything else, but I'm sure he didn't begrudge me my success in America. I'm sad to say a lot did.

'They don't want foreigners who can play—they see it as one place further down the prize list for them, because they're small-minded. It's a hard life and a hard game over there.

'Bobby Locke experienced much the same thing when he went to America in 1947 and started winning tournaments. Eventually the US PGA banned him when, after he won the 1949 Open Championship at Sandwich, he asked to be excused from two American tournaments to which he had previously committed himself because of the demands his Open win made on him. Locke always felt the ban was enforced mainly from jealousy by certain influential players who resented his success.

'Those who make it to the top are a lot purer than those who don't. If I play a guy in match-play and he has a short putt at the last to win, I can't hope he misses his putt. I want to make mine, and if that's not good enough, well fine. The reason I made it is because I think like that. It's the small-minded players of this world who hope that the other person misses a putt. And they are insignificant, so it doesn't matter.

'The fellows who are no good sit around saying, good, Jacko shot 77, Nicklaus shot 80, oh great. But it's the Jackos and Nicklauses who come to the top with free thinking, above all that garbage down below.

'It was necessary to play golf in America, so I went there for a time. But it is also necessary to have a feeling of belonging. The Americans are Americans and we are what we are. I was brought up in a certain way—I mean we're talking about fish and chips, mushy peas, cups of tea, and all that stuff. I like it, I bloody do, and I'm not ashamed of it.

'I can go to America and fall in with everybody, eat steak and salad, I enjoy that. But after a couple of weeks, if someone mentions fish and chips, and mushy peas, I'll go googly eyed, because I like that more. I'm prepared to mix and do my bit, but I do have very strong British ties.

64

Left: *Shades of Harry Vardon. Tony and plus-fours take on the Americans in the 1972 Bing Crosby National Pro-Am at Pebble Beach, California.* Right: *The buggy with the fringe on top. Tony introduces Bradley to the American way of golf.*

'It is important to feel inside you that you belong. I felt like a citizen of the world for a long time, a "cosmopolite". I was brought up with a basic sense of belonging and I need to feel at home in the confines of my house and my two acres in order to keep myself on an even keel. I mix well and like people, but I never felt at home in the United States.

'Most Americans are spoiled rotten – they can't help it. For the most part they think they're camping out if they are playing outside America. They have everything in the world to make life simple and easy: gadgetry, money, cars, freeways, and it spoils them for anywhere else.

'The American interest in golf and in life is based too much on material things. It bugged me. I want nice things, but I put more emphasis on living and enjoying life. Their values are based around a dollar sign, which is not my criterion for a full and happy life.

'These guys are bananas over success, money and power. Much of the Tour is mindless nonsense: it's Hi Frank, Hi Dave, the same thing over and over again. Then all of a sudden you're dead and who cares? Sure I want to be successful – but life is to be savoured as well.

'I love their golf courses. I admire the way they get things done and attain their targets. I would love to play their courses all the time but unfortunately you can't go home for dinner each night from America. If you want to have a marriage and a family life you must compromise. You can say this marriage lark's not very good, and get a divorce like nearly 50 per cent of the American golfers on Tour, whose relationships appear to be shallow. Alternatively, you want to be together.

'Marriage is more important to me because that's going to exist long after golf. The family is forever. Golf is fame and fortune, a five-minute

65

job. When I started out, I saw all the opportunities and said I wanted to be the best golfer in the world. Then my life changed, children came, and there's no point in my kids growing up to 15 and thinking I'm a stranger.

'I've had a lot of pleasure and success out of golf, but it hasn't been close to the pleasure of my family. That's more of a human thing, whereas golf is my job and it's secondary.

'It's a terribly difficult way to make a living in America, grinding it out, week in week out. I would say from the rules they've made that the majority of Americans would prefer to keep their territory to themselves, they resent foreign players on their tour. The rules have all changed over the years. I found that my Open Championship win gave me exemption from qualifying for a year on the US Tour. Prior to my US Open win, everyone got lifetime qualifying exemption, and I don't know when the rule was changed, but I got 10 years. There was a 15 tournament minimum rule which hit foreign players harder, then that was changed in 1978, probably to accommodate Nicklaus who said he was only going to play a dozen tournaments a year. An area qualifying school has been brought in before the main school, and you've almost got to live there for that.

'I know there are a lot of them trying to get out on their Tour and they must protect their own, but then they go out of their way to make a gesture to Severiano Ballesteros and give him a card without his going through the school, because they saw a situation that would reflect well on their Tour and on their Association.

'With all due respect, Australian, Graham Marsh, had done a hell of a lot more than Ballesteros, and he went through the qualifying school and was then left out of the 1978 Masters, which was insulting.

'I gave up my US player's card in 1973 because I thought I could help British golf and I was really always happier playing at home. People were interested in me and I used to go out and play well. I had a huge house in Gloucestershire that I didn't want to leave for six months of the year.

'I was in a unique position. Gary was the only comparison I had with regard to world-travelled players living outside America and playing there. But I was in a totally different position. Gary couldn't have stayed in his own country and played golf as I could, because there just wasn't a year-long alternative tour, so he had to go to America.

'No one had a situation where they could get appearance money and no one had the following of the people that I had–other than Arnold Palmer. Why would I want to play in America when no one gave a hoot?

'In 1973 I won £25,000 in Europe, which was a lot of money at the time. But people said it was no good and I played like a dog. I won the Italian Open and I won the Dunlop Masters by seven shots, but you're supposed to walk that playing one-handed–and it wasn't an Open Championship.

'The British Press build you up and make you feel that all the time you have to be on top form, and it wasn't always possible. In fact it never entered into my thinking that you should sustain that every week.

'I haven't enjoyed my golf as much as I should because I was never allowed to play indifferently by the media. I let it start worrying me; I tried doubly hard and put too much pressure on myself. I was never that good. I was never a Nicklaus. I was Tony Jacklin, who was bloody good on his day and when he'd really got the bit between his teeth, he could take all the pressure people liked to put on him. Technically, maybe I was never 100 per cent. But I had the spirit there – in that I was a player.

'Everything starts to get muddled after winning two Opens, being thrust into the superstar category, being forced to perform well every round. I was torn between playing in America and Britain, between living in England and Jersey. I was running round the world, and it all has to have had an effect in some way. I'm not blaming the situation – just saying it hasn't helped.

'By 1974, although I had won £20,000 in Europe that year, including winning the Scandinavian Open by 11 shots, I started to believe the general opinion that because I wasn't playing in America, my golf was suffering, and I thought I had better go back there – not really because I wanted to, but because I was screwed up.

'I had gained the experience I needed in America in the early years and I didn't have to prove it again. I thought I needed the competition but in the end you've got to play where you want to be. It's more important to win at any level than it is to compete at the highest level.

'In 1975 I went back to America with the whole family – three children, a nanny, the assistant professional from La Moyne golf club in Jersey, who was caddying for me, and we travelled for 15 weeks in a station wagon, like a troop. We rented houses and apartments, and it was awful. I hated it totally. I thought, you've got to give up something to achieve something, but it was almost like a jail sentence to me.

'When you say things like a week seeming a month, that's what it was like. I thought it would never end. I was so miserable that I was in the wrong frame of mind and I couldn't get excited about playing. I didn't know what the hell I wanted. I had compounded my misery by returning.

'I'm glad I went back. I had to return to find out it was wrong. Stubborn bastards like me take a lot of convincing. It's no good someone else telling me, I've got to do it myself. It took some time, because I was going backwards and forwards until the beginning of 1978. Now, I know I would never go back to play in America. I was tossed between two shores for a hell of a long while.

'Nothing would happen if I won another tournament in America, other than that people would say, marvellous, and you re-establish that you're a good player. I've done it in America – nothing can change that. I set out to prove something in America when I was younger, and so far as I'm concerned I've proved it.'

9: Money, Management and Mistakes

MONEY IS A MOTIVATING force in life and so is power. Money can bring power, but the individual is probably attracted more to one than the other. Within Tony Jacklin there is at times an almost insatiable craving for unlimited money which is rooted partly in his childhood insecurities, alternating with a hedonistic pleasure in spending it and a desire to be set apart by having it.

In contrast, American, Mark McCormack, Tony's manager since 1967, appears to be motivated by power which, for him, has been gained partly through money, but more from a desire to pull the strings. McCormack is particularly proud of the fact that through the 1960s he included under his management, without any written contract, Arnold Palmer, Jack Nicklaus and Gary Player.

As British and US Open champion, Tony Jacklin was a fillip for McCormack. But McCormack has come in for some criticism for not guiding Tony more in what he said and did – in terms of his lifestyle after his success, his acquisition of the grand country house, and the fact that he did not tell Tony to be more discreet in what he said on some occasions.

There seems little justification for the criticism, when one is talking of one adult controlling the actions of another. McCormack advised when he was asked. His company probably did make some mistakes along the way – there were, for instance, companies with which Tony became associated which went into liquidation. But that's the risk you take when you go to anyone for advice, they may not always be right.

Tony chose to consult McCormack after his Open Championship victory because he felt McCormack could make him a millionaire.

'A millionaire,' says McCormack, 'is someone who can reduce his assets, such as cash, securities or property, plus his future interests in contracts, to a million pounds.

'If your only asset was a 20-year contract with General Motors, worth $100,000 a year, which would amount to one million pounds over that period of time, then you could take that contract to a bank and get something in return as value. That type of contract, added to liquid assets, determines whether you are a millionaire.

'When people talked of Tony becoming a millionaire, they were talking in terms of contracts entered into solely as a result of his win at Lytham. The contracts that were drawn up, such as those with Pan American, Dunlop, several American golf equipment and clothing contracts, Japanese contracts, others in Britain, some in publishing and in newspapers–

that sum over the length of the contracts equalled a million pounds.

'After Tony's win at Lytham, his victory in the US Open at Hazeltine made him more saleable in America, and it looked like the second step on the rung of a ladder that was going to go a lot higher. The problem has been that it hasn't gone much higher.

'I thought he would be bigger. I held back on negotiating contracts because I thought we might be sorry to sign too soon after Lytham. When he won the US Open I was pleased I had done that–it underlined my opinion. Maybe had we known then what we know now, that he wasn't going to win another major in the next 10 years, the contracts might have been arranged a bit differently. That's the difficult part of the business, trying to judge what a client is going to do and when he will do it. Tony's marketability was on what he was going to do, more than on what he had done.

'Tony's dilemma was being betwixt and between, on wondering do I have enough financial security and a peaceful lifestyle, or should I try the Gary Player rat-race? He opted a little too quickly for the pleasant lifestyle in Britain. Sportsmen tend to have tunnel vision. I almost said some are not very smart. But that's wrong–they are all very smart and most of them are very positive when they are thinking at their best.

'Perhaps when he got to a certain level of success he wasn't hungry enough to win more and more championships at a time when he could have done so. He got hungrier a little later, and then lacked the sparkle in his game to do it.

'I had a varying influence on Tony at varying stages. He asked my opinion a lot after Lytham, when I had a great deal of contact with him and plenty of influence. Today there is not much.

'I'm a great believer that when people earn money they ought to do things that give them pleasure, because otherwise what the hell do you earn it for? To die and give it to some Foundation or to your kids? Tony wanted a house in Gloucester, Arnold wanted a jet, Gary horses. I think it's important these people should do that. I'm not going to resist that kind of thing as long as I feel it is not totally foolhardy and that the cash flow coming in is enough to handle the financial requirements. As it turned out, Tony bought and sold at the wrong times on the property market.

'As for all the other commitments, it is an easy excuse to say that diversification for a sportsman is the reason for doing badly. I've never known anyone who would have won more championships were it not for the fact that their commercial life was so busy.

'Motivation is the real factor. That can be the desire to reach another plateau of accomplishment or the desire to earn more money. But you have to maintain the same killer instinct you had when you were without money. Palmer, Nicklaus and Player all did it.

'I've done it from a sense of wanting to accomplish, wanting to keep going forwards and innovating. I really enjoy what I do. Some people dislike their job–they hate the physical strain of keeping in shape. I try to set a good example by doing what I do, but that's my own thing, what I feel and like. If I didn't like it, I wouldn't do it. Inside, I want success for people I'm associated with, in varying degrees. I either want a particular client to win something because I really want him to succeed, or because I like him. Maybe I feel that I can make a lot of money from it or it is some combination of them all.

'There are people who you want to win, no matter what. Arnold Palmer, by winning the US PGA Championship, would not make a dollar difference to me, but I'd really like him to do that because I know how much it would mean to him.

'I want Tony to succeed in the same way as I want Palmer to succeed. I like Tony a lot. He's the kind of person with whom, if we had time, I would have fun spending a week together somewhere, playing golf, tennis and swimming.

'I think that with Tony the British Press overdid it. The man had a cold and the *Daily Express* would say, "Jacko has Cold" or "Jacko Sneezes at Tucson". Jesus, it's ridiculous. It's the British method indigenous to the British Press, whereas the American Press is more interested in results, not the person. The British Press gets a hero, and then anything he does, they write, because they figure that's what the reader wants to know. The *New York Times* would never have said Arnold Palmer had a cold.

'Tony had a compressed success. He had and still has immense charisma and through this he is able to get more out of a little success than others can out of a lot. I do think–and have constantly maintained–that he'll come back. He's young enough; it's just a question of getting it all together. We haven't heard the last of him.'

For Tony, money was tight in his childhood and the cost of everything was always discussed at home but his was not a real rags-to-riches story, more a desire for the good things in life.

'I was 80 per cent motivated by money, although originally the money didn't matter. I was side-tracked by it, which happened with success. Money draws you.

'When I was a kid I never had any pocket money. I never had new things. My first new bike was when I went on the TV Superstars show and they gave us the bikes we had used. I was 28 years old. Not that I wanted a bike then–I gave it to my Dad because he got banned from driving and it meant he could cycle to work.

'I never had new golf clubs until after I turned professional. My Dad always talked about money–you had to have it. We always had a little car–a banger–while other families who earned what we did didn't have one. We went without other things to have it and, in retrospect, it wasn't bad. Ever since I can remember, I took the papers out and earned 10 shil-

Bert Yancey, Tony's close friend on the US Tour, playing during the 1973 Open at Troon.

Tom and Jean Weiskopf celebrate 1973 Open Championship victory at Troon.

lings a week, part of that went on a seven-pence frame at the snooker-hall, part on cigarettes.

'Then suddenly you get to a point where you can look in a shop-window and say I like that, I'll have it. You can't imagine the feeling you get when you can do that. I've enjoyed money, I've spent enough, and since I've had it I've never wanted for anything.

'If my old man were in a restaurant and the steak was tough, or if you were full up, it wouldn't make any difference–you'd have to eat it, you couldn't leave it because he or someone else would be paying for it.

'In America, I'd be sitting with a couple of fellows before tee-off time and we'd have a Coke, throw five dollars on the table, and a guy would take a sip out of his glass, then someone would call him away and he would go, leaving the whole drink. I would never do that–I couldn't. I've sat at night and thought about it. You buy a drink, take it with you, it's been poured and it's yours. I wish I were more the other way because then I wouldn't be so conscious of money.

'Money bothers me and I'm well off. I haven't got as much as I think I should have, but then who has? I don't make fortunes on the Stock Market. My money has been earned playing golf tournaments, and from the companies I represent. Deep down I know I'll survive, but I'm still basically an insecure person about money.

'If I lost everything tomorrow, I know darned well that I would figure out something to do to start it all up again. I'd hate to have to do it but there's no way I'd be happy just existing–I want to live. I'm the sort of fellow who could go back to a semi-detached, fish and chips, and start looking for something else to do to make money. I used to think it would be great to retire but now I think it would be the most boring thing in the world.

'I know there are certain things all the money in the world can't buy. I've had a good life but I want to be very wealthy–I'd like to be a millionaire and I'm not. It's just a personal thing. Probably I never will be in my terms. A millionaire to me is being able to put your hands on a cool million–£350,000 to £400,000 is bugger-all. I've always got a few thousand quid put by, which I'd like to think is enough, but it isn't. I'm money conscious but not mean. I love nice things and I want security because that is important to me.

'I'd like enough money to have my own jet. I'd like money to the point where they can say what they like about you, but it doesn't matter, because you've got so much. I want a tremendous amount of money so that I would never have to stand in line for anything, or go when someone tells me I've got to. I'd like to do what I want, when I want to do it.

'Like Frank Sinatra, who gets out the DC9, collects up his entourage and then it's–let's go to London. You 'phone in to the airport and Customs is ready to handle you; you're ushered off into a limousine, there's no hassle, no waiting for bags or talking to people.

Right: *Tony's manager, Mark McCormack, the most powerful man in sport.* Centre: *Tony practises bunker shots at Winchcombe.* Bottom: *'Tis my delight on a Friday night' The Lincolnshire Poacher?*

'If anyone wants to know something, you have a Press Conference, then you've got total privacy wherever you are. Crowded public places aggravate me. Maybe I'm a dreamer, but if I hadn't been, I wouldn't have got this far.

'Money doesn't bring happiness but it's a hell of a lot easier to be rich and happy than poor and happy – providing you have a set of values. I'm not such a dreamer that I think if I had 10 million quid, life would be a breeze. There would still be problems.

'In the early days, George Blumberg from South Africa offered to talk to someone about managing my affairs and, although I didn't know it at the time, it was Mark McCormack. I joined him in 1967 when Arnold Palmer, Gary Player, Jack Nicklaus, Doug Sanders and Bob Charles were all with him.

'McCormack rang up and we had a meeting in London. He said, if you want me to represent you, the deal is 20 per cent down the line on everything. We feel we give a good service, but you suit yourself. We shook hands, never signed a contract, and he said, I hope you make a million, because if you do, the chances are I will.

'A couple of weeks later I won the Dunlop Masters at Sandwich. At that time, I was playing mostly in America and in 1968 I won the Jacksonville Open. Then after winning the British Open in 1969, it all began to happen. I knew I was supposed to make a fortune – and I did. I suppose over the years I have made a million pounds out of golf but I probably haven't got half of it. I worked my arse off for it, I ran myself into the ground. Nothing's for nothing.

'When I won the Open, I had bought a house a few months before, at Elsham in Lincolnshire, for £10,800, which was a lot of money at that time. It was a nice four-bedroomed house and we set about doing things to it. I won the Open before we finished and ended up spending £11,200 on it. We lived in it for three years and sold it in 1972 for £22,000.

'It was marvellous living there. I love it as an area – I grew up there, but it was impractical. I was always going on a four-hour drive to London Airport and I wanted to be closer than that.

'So I bought Winchcombe in Gloucestershire which was only two hours from the airport. Our nearest neighbour was half a mile away – it was great. The house had 33 rooms – it was old stone and very attractive with a tiered garden. There were three cottages and I employed six people living in them.

'We put fitted carpets right through the house, best velvet curtains and had hand-made Spanish furniture. We made bedroom, bathroom and dressing room suites everywhere. We redesigned the kitchen and family room.

'I built an indoor swimming pool for £20,000 with a fireplace at one end. I added a sauna and solarium. In the garden, I had a practice putting green, bunkers, and a fairway where I could hit a full drive. I didn't spend that kind of money willy-nilly – I anticipated living there for a long time. At that point, the economy had not blown and there was no indication that inflation would go berserk.

'I suppose one of the feelings I got about the house was the fact that you live in an old place like that and wonder who lived there before you and whether you were keeping up the tradition in the way it was supposed to be done. The sad part of those places comes when people can no longer live in them in the manner to which they had formerly been accustomed. I'm a bit big on the fact that it should be done the right way.

'It was marvellous. I lived in the grand manner and I enjoyed it. I didn't enjoy employing all the people we needed to run the house – there was always someone around – it was like Paddington Station in the mornings at breakfast – which means there is a lack of privacy. Then you get to know all their problems, it all comes back to you, and it's a pain in the arse – in the end the buggers are running your life.

'In November 1974 there was a new Labour Government, following which a new tax law came into effect, making world income taxable in the United Kingdom even if you left it outside the UK. That meant my American and Japanese earnings would be taxed in Britain. So I said stick it. I would go anywhere to avoid that.

'People can think what the hell they like about my leaving – it doesn't bother me. I'm not going to work my arse off to finish with bugger-all. If I'd stayed in England and earned £100,000, I would have kept around £18,000 after tax, which was no good to me. The wages bill alone at Winchcombe was about £500 a week.

'People say you should stay and pay taxes, and I always did – I paid a lot on what I earned in Britain. Then I went to other countries, created a lot of income away from Britain because I was motivated to go there, and there's no way I'm going to pay British tax on that. I would still be living here now if that tax law hadn't changed. I don't hold it against anyone but the system disappointed me. I could still live in England, but then I would cheat like everyone else cheats the Government. If you pay the proper amount of income tax you can't afford to run round in a Jaguar, but plenty of people do and everyone accepts cheating as a way of life. It's sick.

'When I was told about the tax situation, I was able to turn my back on Winchcombe and just walk away from it. I've never thought about it since. I can honestly say it didn't bother me at all. It was sad because we spent so much time and money on it and I didn't want it to end so abruptly. But quite frankly, if you said now – you can have it back – I wouldn't want it.

'The problem with Winchcombe was that it was so huge and although I wanted to live like that, I found you couldn't in this day and age. You need to be titled to find the help with the amount of respect necessary to run an establishment like that. There's not that sort of respect left among the English working classes–they don't want to be subservient. And I don't want that relationship either. I sold the house in 1975 for £110,000, having bought it three years previously for £120,000 and having spent £70,000 on it. Then we moved to Jersey.

'I could have been better advised. If someone in the McCormack organisation had been strong enough to say do you really know what you are doing–I probably could have been talked out of it. You may give the impression you are strong, but we all need a shoulder to lean on at times when we flounder a bit.

'Sure I wanted the place, but it was too big, we could have got it for less, and they should have looked deeper into my financial situation. When I won the Open, I told Mark that more than anything else I wanted my future assured. Why wasn't Jersey suggested at that stage? But you do these things, they're part of living and I don't regret Winchcombe. No one else in sport in England will ever live in the same grand manner as I did for three years.

'From 1968 my annual income was over £50,000. In 1970 and 1971 it went up to about £200,000 annually for those two years. As quickly as I made it, I had it taken off me in tax. I made about a million dollars in three years and found it's not what you make, it's what you keep that is important. I made the money, and I wasn't forced to have the big house, but after the whole thing is over it's far from being as attractive as the Press try to make out. All you get out of £200,000 is about £40,000 to spend, which is not bad money, but when you're running round in Rolls-Royces and living in a mansion–it goes quickly.

'I was always mad about cars, I've had more than 30 of them. I had my first Aston Martin DB5 in 1969, which was one of the best cars ever–I wish I could have it back now. I kept it a year and some berk told me a Jensen was better. I got a four-wheel drive Jensen with every attachment on it and pranged it after a week. I wrote it off going round a corner too fast near Elsham Golf Club. Then I bought a Rolls-Royce, a marvellous Silver Cloud in blue, with white upholstery, and a TJ 65 number plate. I kept that a year and ordered another to my specifications in gold and black, with an interior gold carpet. I thought it would be just as good as the first one, but it wasn't, and I kept that for a year. After that, I bought an old 1965 Bentley Continental–I had it all re-upholstered, resprayed, and after 10 months decided I didn't like it. I then had a Mercedes 450SEL, which I think was the best car I ever had–I really enjoyed it. Then when we moved to Jersey, I sold it, and we've had a series of cars since then, as part of a deal I have with Avis.

'Japan was one of my major sources of income–not that I did very well playing golf there–but you don't realise how crazy they are on the sport. I would walk through a department store in Japan, and people would stop and say: "Ah so–it's Jacklin." They know all the golfers and I was a big name in Japan.

'I had a shirt contract which was worth $5,000 plus royalties and the first year the royalties on the contract came in at $55,000. McCormack's office sent a telex back asking if there had been some mistake–and there hadn't. There was a terrific amount of money to be made in Japan and it was thanks to McCormack's operation being there, that I could take advantage of it. Those royalties went on for about four or five years.

'Another lucrative contract was with Pan American–worth $30,000 a year for three years–for which I was supposed to play golf with customers and travel agents in America on occasions, and I think I did play about twice.

'In appearance money, I could get $10,000 a day for playing an exhibition in Japan, and about the same plus prize money in a Japanese tournament. In most British tournaments I received about £2,000. I have often been paid to play and then played badly, and you feel you haven't earned the money. On the other hand, most sponsors are in it for the publicity, which is what they get–because whether I played well or badly, I was still written about. And the people still came out to watch even if I put up an indifferent performance.

'Certain of the media say he gets his £2,000 and doesn't care how he plays. That's bull because you'd never have made it in the first place if you didn't care. You don't become a champion by accident. A great deal of hard work and dedication goes into it. Coupled with that, there's an honesty to oneself that is necessary. You never feel good about playing badly, especially when you're being paid. Latterly, I made arrangements at tournaments on an incentive basis–so that I got paid the full amount if I played well. It made me feel better.

'After the 1969 Open, I was working very hard, playing between 15 and 22 tournaments in America, as well as tournaments in Australia, Japan and Europe. I ran myself into the ground. I would never do it again if I won another Open–I learned a lesson.

'I remember on one occasion, when I was US Open champion, I played an exhibition in Kansas City. Some character was up for local election and, as part of his campaign, he arranged for 72 guys to be out on the golf course–there was a four-ball on every tee waiting to play one hole with me. I had to go from hole to hole shaking hands and playing with everybody. I got $4,000 for it. I said to McCormack, never ever do that to me again. I felt like a prostitute.

'My club contract was one that I signed in 1969 with Dunlop for a 10-year period. The worst thing was that there was no inflation clause. Royalties were between five and six per cent on club sales, and the contract brought in from £5,000 to £10,000 a year.

'I played a lot in America, but never had a US contract with them. They were prepared to see me go and play the same set in America as in England, and never offer me any extra. Why should they? I was playing their clubs anyway–I won the US Open playing them.

'I had joined Dunlop in the early days when I was with Bill Shankland at Potters Bar because that was his company. Eric Hays at Dunlop had helped me with £200 to go to South Africa, which I paid back by working it into a deal.

'After 1969, I used to go to the Dunlop factory to give advice on the new Tony Jacklin model that was produced every three years. I remember vividly in 1972 telling them that the present shape of the head of the club needed to be altered to look more attractive and expensive. It was currently red, white and blue, which I said might be patriotic but not too attractive. They listened to all the points I made then I walked round the factory and had my photo taken with the workers to give them a boost.

'The next new autographed model of my clubs came out exactly the same as it was before. But the Dunlop Maxfli model was black and gold, which was exactly what I had suggested mine should be. I called McCormack straight away and said I wanted my clubs withdrawn from the market and my name taken off them. All hell was let loose.

'My clubs were withdrawn and they put them back on the market in black and gold. Following that, I got a polite letter from Dunlop telling me not to interfere in future. The point was that nothing I ever said mattered. It didn't take me long to realise that all they wanted was my name on the clubs, hoping it would sell them.

'Eventually, I told McCormack that I wanted to get out of the Dunlop contract. He said it would be difficult, but I didn't care, I wanted out.

'I started playing Ping clubs in America in 1975 and Dunlop back home. At that time, Ping paid you $600 just to play their clubs in a tournament. If you were well placed, you got more – it was on an incentive basis. I was making $1,000 a week playing Ping, which wasn't bad.

'In 1978 I changed back again to my Dunlop clubs as I decided I liked them better and I'm more used to them. I know I hit them properly and I've been successful with them. I haven't any contract but I don't care about the money. If I win tournaments the money will come.

'When I won the Open Championship, Mark McCormack did all my deals personally for me. I saw a lot of him and we got on fine. Arnold has always been number one with Mark, and always will be – he's his closest friend – but we used to see more of each other.

'Then he got bigger and bigger and I don't see him now. He works harder than ever, but he delegates more. He's a good businessman. You can say these people are leeches – on the other hand, he's a guy who sees an opportunity to do a job for somebody else, he does it, and he has to get paid for doing it.

'I like Mark. If he'd ever slow down for long enough, he's the sort of bloke I'd like as a friend. He hasn't got time for friends though, apart from Arnold. People are associates – he doesn't make friends.

'I like his integrity and very few people have a lot of integrity. Mark has always been very honest. The world is full of weak people who are quite prepared to sit back, watch and criticise a guy like that. Somehow Mark manages to do the right thing more often than not. Everyone is out for his scalp–that's the price he pays for being as good as he is at what he does. He's weathered the storm over a long period of time.

'The majority of people who criticise him are jealous, like the ones who criticise me for leaving the country because of tax problems. They're insanely jealous and wish they earned enough to do it themselves. In my experience we're all selfish and all out for one person–ourself. McCormack is out for himself but he's realised he's had to bend and weave a little along the way.

'The McCormack organisation generates a good income from contracts. The one thing that I didn't accept from the organisation was that from 1972 I didn't get the service I thought was right. I'm a reasonable fellow and I accept they can't do everything for me all the time. They can't work miracles and you are only as good as you play. But in raw numbers, if you're making £100,000 or more a year, you're paying a minimum of £20,000 of that to them, and they should do something for it.

'They kept having staff changes and in 1975 I got so pissed off I said that McCormack could have 25 per cent of what he made me, but he wouldn't get anything of what I got for myself. I did that for a few months and then found I was left out of things and it became very difficult because they lost interest in me. I was never happy with the situation and did it as a gesture to tell McCormack I was unhappy. Now I get good service from the organisation.

'My income over the last few years has been in the region of £100,000 annually. They say the first £10,000 is the worst, but that's bull. You invest it wrongly and it all goes. You know that no matter how much money you make, you spend it, or someone else does for you. It's scary how much you can make and how you can lose it.

'That's partly the reason I now live in Jersey, but if I ever won another Open I wouldn't buy a bigger house. I blew about £100,000 out of taxed income, which was a lot of money, on a house and living in it for three years. I'm going to be careful with my money in future.

'If I thought I've done all I have with all the worry, practice, travel, and the things I've given up through the past 10 years, only to find I wasn't going to have anything at the end, other than the memory, I would die. It would be the worst feeling in the world. It would be like saying, Go Back to Jail, Do Not Pass Go, Do Not Collect £200–start again. My God, maybe that's what I need, perhaps I should go back to the beginning.'

10: The Inner Conflict

BY THE END OF the 1977 golf season Tony was at a low ebb and still thrashing around uncomfortably in a depression, although no one had ever suggested or acknowledged this fact.

When, as a top-level sportsman, you become unable to perform at your particular sport, the chances are that you are either reacting to a low state brought about perhaps by over-exposure, or you may slide into a depression through an accumulation of circumstances that become extremely painful, particularly when you continue to subject yourself week in and week out to the very thing at which you are unable to succeed.

It is possible that you may play yourself out of a depression or low state of mind, and regard it as just being a bad spell. On the other hand, when disaster compounds itself to the extent that you can no longer produce the desired results because the effort has become too great, then it is clear that the pace has proved too fast–the mind and body have reached an exhausted state.

It was not that 1977 was a complete disaster, far from it. In January, Tony was competing on the American Tour and played very well at Tucson, where he was in contention in the last round and finished tied 18th. The following week he raised his game to come second to Tom Watson in the Bing Crosby tournament at Pebble Beach, where he and many others were disappointed not to see him the winner. He took six up the final hole and Watson pipped him to the post by one shot.

Because of his relatively low-key performance over the previous few years, the element of doubt crept in concerning his ability to handle the big occasion and subconsciously Tony allowed himself to be affected. He maintained, however, that his club choice of a one iron, instead of a driver, off the 18th tee at Pebble Beach in the final round of the Crosby, was one that he would not change given the moment again.

At the end of the season Tony won the English Professionals' Championship, which was dismissed lightly as containing little competition. This is never true since to win a four-round tournament you have to play well as there is always someone in the field who can have a great week or great round and beat you. Nick Job, with a 66 on the last day, nearly did just that. Neither the Press nor Tony put too much store by his win. He was not, he said, enjoying his golf due to his continued putting problems.

So far as Tony was concerned his state of mind all revolved around his putting, since this was the one area in his game over which he had no control and which was causing him so much pain. 'I felt like quitting in

1977 – I definitely thought, who needs the aggravation? There's a differ-ence between doing something unpleasant each day or feeling like you were shackling yourself and letting some bastard whip you. I was hurting myself and not just doing something I disliked. It was taking so much out of me, there was no point, it became stupid. I really wasn't playing golf. As soon as I walked on to the tee the shutters came down and I didn't enjoy anything. I was waiting for all the bad things to happen, waiting for the situation where I knew that I would have a putt and get myself worked up into such a state about it that I couldn't hit it, or at least when I did it would go sideways. I just felt there was no way I could get the putter through. I could always take it away but I couldn't control the path of it coming through – my hands would go. I tried all sorts of positions and the last thing I was thinking about was holing the putt, which should be the first thing to think of instead of my obsession with putting a good stroke on it.

'People were writing to tell me what I should do with my putting but I couldn't do what anyone suggested. Anyway I know more about the golf game than 99.9 per cent of the guys out there, especially the amateurs. I've played with all the great players. I've dissected the game, I know what a strike is, whether my hands are too low, too high, too far back; all about rhythm, timing, weight, and eye over the ball. Christ, I had hundreds of letters and none of it was to the point. What these people didn't under-stand was the fact that I knew all the time, but it was a question of getting on a green and doing it – because it was between my ears, my mind wouldn't let me do it.

'I've always had the most vivid dreams about golf, and they were not good either. I would hit the ball and it would go into a sink. There I am in a washbasin, and the ball is sitting in the plug-hole. Then I'm in the sink trying to get the club back, but I can't because the sink is too curved. I have to get it out of the plug-hole and finally I wake up in frustration trying to do it.

'In another dream I've putted, and the ball goes under a wardrobe, and there I am flashing about with my putter, trying to get it out from under the wardrobe.

'Then I was playing golf with my Dad, and someone threw a ball from behind a hedge and said, hit this one, it's a good one. The ball was called a "Missileite", and when you hit it, the ball went forever – like a missile.

'On another occasion I was playing with some other guys and hitting off a tee. There were sliding aluminium doors in front of the tee and they were open when the other fellows hit, but when it came to my turn they closed the doors until they were only a foot apart. I had to tee off and I was thinking, shit, I've got to get through that little gap.

'In one dream I had, I couldn't swing the club back because there was a wall behind me, so that I couldn't generate enough clubhead speed to hit the ball.

82

'Usually I dream during tournaments but never about winning–my dreams all are on the negative side.'

'It may sound stupid but I couldn't think through the barrier–it was as though someone had just put a block there. I was terrified every time I stepped up to a putt. The rest of my game was so natural because I never thought about it–only what happened on the putting green. However well I played it meant nothing in relation to my score. It was a fight, an effort, just like an ice wall and there's no way to get over it. That's what I was up against every time I walked on to a green. I got to the point that when I was over a six-inch putt I visualised muffing it, I couldn't knock the ball in smoothly. Every single part of every game was an effort because I had a conflict between a will to want to do it and an almost bigger will not allowing me to do it. It was desperate. I thought putting was the most important thing in the whole world and, honest to God, I wondered if I were sane. I would say to myself why on earth do I want to put myself through this anguish and torment all the time when it seemed that nothing good ever happened. It was just miserable.'

Tony's misery over his putting and mental problems finally made him recall a woman, now around 50, whom he had met in South Africa in 1965 and 1966, named Réné Kurunsky. He searched out and found an old letter from Réné with her telephone number in Johannesburg and he picked up the 'phone and dialled it. 'A native girl answered and told me she would be back later so I knew she was still there. When I got through again, she said, "Tony, my Tony what's up"–just like that after 12 years. I told her I was desperate with my game and she had been the only one who had really helped me when I was playing in South Africa all those years ago and my putting had been terrible. She had told me I was allowing myself to build barriers and worrying too much. She said that if I didn't stay in the present, I would go into a low and worry about the past or future. Réné told me to look at trees, at my feet moving, to make myself aware of the present. It was commonsense and it worked. Being positive, you are what you think you are, you will win if you set out to win, you can do anything with a firm belief in your ability.

'I've always known I had the ability, although it can stagnate and waste if you misuse it, and now I'd got all the channels blocked. During my depression I had all this ability within me and I wouldn't let it come out. You want to burst and there's no way you can relax enough to allow it to happen, you're so uptight.

'The first thing Réné said to me on the telephone was, what are you trying to do when you get on a green? Trying to make a good stroke I replied, and she said that's bull for a start. You're supposed to get the ball in the hole aren't you? So why don't you try to do that instead of making a good stroke? That was the first indication to me that I'd been barking up the wrong tree, that I'd got myself into such a state and so blind, I never even realised my objectives were wrong.'

It just so happens that René Kurunsky is a Scientologist. After the telephone call, and after trying a new approach to putting, Tony decided, on her recommendation, that he would spend a few days at the College of Scientology, founded by American, Ron Hubbard, at East Grinstead, Sussex. In November 1977, he spent about £1,000 for Vivien and himself to go along and be 'audited'. Impatient by nature, Tony tried to run the sessions, to tell them he hadn't any problems other than his putting. Tony's personality does not allow him to admit to any weakness or chink in his armour, and with such people, self-analysis can prove very painful. But finally the treatment began to work, the concentration and attention accorded him were attractive. 'I liked to do an hour's session every day,' Tony admits indulgently. Then with more practical sense: 'But it's a joke what they charge. I thought it was extortionate, nothing more nor less— it worked out at £25 per hour. But I think they've got something going there, whatever it is.

'I sat in a room with a woman–she doesn't tell you anything, you explain yourself in the end and they ask you questions. It's very clever–actually it's marvellous, it really is. She asked me all sorts of questions about my early life and my parents–all bull–any problems I may have had I accept in that regard. For instance, if I had arguments when I was growing up it didn't bother me, nothing bothered me. I never lay in bed worrying or got frustrated about it. I thought all the questions were leading up to something but they weren't. So I protested and said this is all bull, I'm doing nothing but talking, you're writing all sorts of notes and I'm getting nowhere. I want to get on to the areas where I can benefit and that's on the golf course where my thinking is bad.

'So they sent another woman who asked me what bothered me most, and I replied my putting. She asked what happens, and we went into all that, and even though you're talking to non-golfers it doesn't make any difference. They love their job these women. It's a very interesting job with the mind–to ask the right questions in order to get the answers you want.

'I went into another session with the first woman and she told me to imagine all the things that could happen on a putting green. So I went through a list of about 20 things, like, it could get dark when you walk onto it; the hole could heal up; it could get windy or rain; the grass could turn blue. She kept saying yes, and eventually I said, well you can imagine anything can't you–the ultimate answer. Straight away she says, thank you. And you realise the fact that this is the whole point, you can imagine anything, good, bad or indifferent and I was imagining the worst of every-thing. When you're as low as I was you forget all about the good side. Then that session finished.

'Next, I was asked what is your problem? Well I can't putt. What part of your problem can't you face? Well I can face any part of it. I know, but what part can't you face? Any part I replied, and again the same question.

Then you start delving deeper into your mind and ultimately I said, well I'm negative and she said, thank you.

'You won't admit that to yourself, but having done so it did me a power of good. I came away from there feeling so much more aware of every aspect of everything. Although the woman drove me bananas at times and it pissed me off the hours I spent, I enjoyed it because you use your own mind. What does postulate mean? she said. I'd say, well . . . and then she gave me a dictionary and told me to look it up . . . it means to imagine you can–postulate you are going to win this tournament.

'The belief in Scientology is that we're all a spirit first. Réné always reckons I've got a fantastic spirit which makes me what I am. Your spirit is your soul–a *thetan*–and it goes on, and has gone on forever. It is in your body which will die, and it will go on. There are certain things in your mind you can't fully explain, thinking maybe it's happened before, or deep, deep things that are almost too much to believe they happened in your lifetime. Children, when they say things to you, sometimes have an understanding deeper than is possible. If you accept that the spirit goes on, the mind is just meat and believes what it is fed. The spirit is the person and the mind can get in the way.

'The problem is that sportsmen need to be more childlike because there's no fear in children. The same as if I want to throw something I throw it naturally, I don't have to think about it, I let it go. When we're childlike and let it happen rather than make it happen, that's when it will happen right. My reaction to what had been fed into my mind had affected my thinking, my clarity, but I benefited immediately I admitted I was negative.

'With Severiano Ballesteros I can feel and sense when I'm near him that he is thinking totally clearly–there's no purpose other than getting the ball into the hole. Maybe that will change with the years, with experience and happenings, or maybe he'll retain it and understand what makes it happen as he develops. Jack is probably the only one who has done that. Gary is close too.

'In Scientology you are forced to use areas of your mind that have lain dormant. I read a lot and know most words, but the most important thing is never to use a word you don't fully understand. While we were at the College, we weren't allowed to drink and you're supposed to have seven hours' sleep a night and never go hungry. I felt fantastic after five hours' auditing a day for four days, not just about my problem, but I was so aware of everything.

'Viv went though she had no need to go, but they said it's nice if she does and she did life repair. She didn't need it, she's as happy as Larry, she could ask them questions, but she enjoyed it. At the end they tried to get me to go on another course, but I thought, look out, they're getting their claws into you. I'm a pro golfer not a Scientologist, so I didn't want to get involved. But I've never seen a happier bunch of people who sometimes work 12 to 14 hours a day. Scientology means the "knowledge of wisdom". Ron Hubbard was the founder and he's been knocked like any individual who wants to be different. He may be right or he could be wrong, but he's a bloody smart cookie.

'When I went to the College, or Saint Hill as they call it, I thought there would be a magic answer. A lot of it's a waste of time. I waffled on about every damned thing that came into my head and none of it was relevant. I'm the happiest guy in the world with healthy kids, a marvellous wife, a lovely home, comfortably off, healthy and fit. But I really enjoyed digging into my mind–I got a natural high from it. The only other time I felt anything like it was playing at Dalmahoy, when I won the Wills Open by seven shots, and in one round I felt that I could put the ball wherever I wanted. I shot 65 and putted like a fool, but I was on a higher level of concentration and it was fantastic.

'Ron Hubbard is incredible. The millions of words he has written mean he's putting down in black and white the finer feelings that I would have. He's using all the right words that I wouldn't begin to know, but had I taken a different path I would like to have been that clever–to be able to put on paper in a logical, sensible way, exactly the things that one feels. He's more right than anything I've read, or am likely to believe in.

'Writing this book on Tony Jacklin will take hours and hours to put together, and then people will interpret it exactly how they wish. Why can't they read what is written? Scientology is reading the absolute and understanding all of it.

'Anxiety takes you into the past, says Ron Hubbard. The important thing is that you've got to think about the past in order to be anxious. I don't suppose most people would think in those terms and sometime in my life I may be able to help someone else. When you get anxious, it's because of something that has happened before. In golf terms, you become anxious about a shot because you know all the variables.

'When I was at my lowest ebb, gaining that knowledge was an important factor, an aid to helping me out of it. It gave me a greater understanding of my problem–and there was no question that I did have a problem.

'In my bad spell I sometimes criticised myself and would think others were lucky, which was bad. I should have been doing something else to get my mind straightened out.

'I'm not a religious person, but Scientology is as close as anything I've come to that I would believe in concerning the spirit that is in every individual.

'Take the Bible–it's a marvellous fairy tale. It's just a great story of good, giving indications to everyone how good God is, Jesus is, and the fact that all these marvellous stories should make you pure. The stories all have morals but I think they are open to many interpretations.

'Everybody needs to believe in something. If they haven't a strong belief in themselves, they need something else to hang on to. They are lectured by preachers and priests in a search for inner comfort.

'I believe in something – maybe it's me, and someone will say, you selfish bastard. Well I'm sorry, but that's the way I am. Young people are apt to try to beat the world, and if you're not selfish and trying to do that one thing, you'll be eaten. You may wear a few different hats, but life is for the takers.

'It's not just myself that I believe in, it's more than that but it's difficult to define – maybe it's a superior being. I don't know whether anyone knows what it is.

'I know when you're dead, you're dead, and that's it, forget it.' What will happen is that the soul is the memory that one leaves behind. Whether you go out with a machine gun and murder people, or you lead a good life, isn't going to make a scrap of difference as to whether you go to heaven or hell. Going to hell means that everyone you have left behind thinks you've gone there.

'I'll never be blotted out, will I? I'd like to think I was going to get my three score years and ten, but if I died tomorrow I wouldn't regret any-thing. There's nothing at this stage of my life that I wish I had done. It would bother me if someone died and had not known the full value of knowledge, fun and experience in their life, because I think every human being deserves the chance to take it.

'But after you've done everything and maybe become a genius, you have to remember you're flesh and blood, and people die – that's the only inevitable thing. As long as you live your life with that knowledge, you can't be too disappointed when it happens.'

11: Friendship and the Weiskopfs

IN TERMS OF HAVING friends of his own age, Tony has perhaps never been that close to anyone, although others may have felt close to him. As to friendships when he was a youngster he comments, 'I had no great friends, I just played golf every day.' When he went into professional golf he teamed up with fellow assistant professional, Richard Emery, to play other people for money, to supplement their meagre income. Then he sometimes roomed with professional, Alex Caygill, for their first tournaments. But Tony says of friendships in golfing circles: 'You don't get very close to other professional golfers because really there's a barrier.

'I get disappointed by people, possibly because I expect too much. There are not that many people you can really rely on and when you do find someone he automatically becomes your friend or ally. I haven't any dubious friends. The people I call friends are reliable. There are very few people who come up to those standards to become good friends.

'I find it difficult to meet people who have seen the things I've seen. I'm not getting on my high horse, but golf has taken me around the world a dozen times and I've met a fantastic cross-section of important people. I've talked to them about life and their views and I've sat round the table and got into deep conversations.

'You form your own conclusions that life is what you make it and you are what you want to be. Most people are content with the daily drudgery, and if that's what they want it's fine. The type of people I've met want a bit more. They see life as being quite exciting. I'm prepared to give more in a relationship than the majority of people. If someone were my friend, I'd do anything for him, anything. Very few are prepared to do that.

'I have a very good friend in Norfolk, a farmer called John Greetham, whom I've known for a long time. Basically we see life the same way and we have the same priorities even though we disagree on some things. We have great chats together. He's a great one, as I am, for doing your sums, for taking stock of your life.

'Every now and then, however good or bad it is, an individual should sit back and take stock of his life. What have you got? What would you like to put right? What are your ambitions? And when you're a bit down, you should look at the plus factors.

'I've travelled with John for three weeks at a time, and it's difficult to be with someone that long without feeling they're getting on your nerves. But he never does and we get on well together.

'I've enjoyed friendships with two guys, one in Los Angeles and one in

Johannesburg, who both had a great sense of humour and a fantastic wealth of experience–and both died recently aged 64. I always went for older people when it came to wanting to know something. They were two guys I could call friends. They hadn't anything to gain from knowing me–there was just the pleasure of each other's company. Then they died. I'll never forget them.

'I met Irv Raskin in California in 1968 and whenever I went to Los Angeles, wherever I was staying, he would pick me up every morning and we would go to a delicatessen called Nate and Al's for breakfast. I knew everyone there, although I only went once a year for a week. I used to have lox and begels and it was fantastic.

'Irv worked at a radio station and did all sorts of other things too. He was always out to make his million–he never quite did, and then he died of a heart attack in 1977. We had lots of deep conversations. People don't talk enough, certainly not men. There are some aspects of life about which men feel too embarrassed to discuss. They're not sexual things–just emotional–about your family, your job or anything. For some individuals it's a weakness to talk about something that really upsets them emotionally. Because of their experience, older people realise there isn't any sense in not talking about emotional problems.

'When I went to South Africa in 1965 I met Danny Martin in Johannesburg and stayed with him, and again when I was there in 1966 I was at his place. He was fantastic and everyone loved him. He had been through the mill, but he maintained this incredible child-like quality that adults usually lose, but Danny never lost it. That's why I was so attracted to him.

'He was a kid really, he had funny sayings and saw the funny side of everything. We spent night after night yarning and gagging. I talked to him about the mind, his spirit was so strong, he was one of the great people. He made steel for the sides of refrigerators and washing machines and if he had wanted to make a million he would have done so.

'When you're around someone who has a genuine sense of humour, who sees life as a fun game and means it, then it really makes you feel good, that life is a ball whatever happens and however you're playing golf, it's fun to be alive. Danny had the ability to make people feel that.

'He died of cancer in April 1978, and the world's worse off for losing a guy like that. It broke me up–but he's not dead, only for our purposes–guys like him can't die. He left too much behind.'

'When I was at Potters Bar I made two very good friends, Johnnie Rubens and Wally Dubabney and their friendship has stayed with me since then.'

When he went to America he became one of a trio–Bert Yancey, Tom Weiskopf and Tony Jacklin. All three had tremendous potential and it was Tony who first achieved major status, followed by Tom. Bert Yancey had been winning on the US Tour since 1966, when, in his third season, he won three tournaments. Yancey's best financial year was in 1974 when he won $84,692, though as early as 1967 he had been 13th on the money list. In 1975 he cracked up, became really ill, was finally diagnosed as a manic depressive and the effect of the drugs he needed ended his days of competitive golf. In the early days, Tom and his wife Jean, Bert and Linda Yancey, Tony and Vivien, shared much of their life together on Tour.

'I was friendly with Tom and Bert, and we basically had the same views regarding golf. The Americans as a whole are far more professional than we are–it's a harder school. I had that in common with Tom and Bert, we all knew how tough it was. If one of us shot a good round in a tournament, you knew how difficult it was on the golf course. We had common outlooks on the integrity of a professional golfer.

'But my life was very different from theirs–my background, my lifestyle and the things I enjoyed. Over and above the golf and surrounding activities, we did not share much else. We visited each other, enjoyed sharing the other's way of life for short periods, and that was it. That is the case with all my American acquaintances.

'When I first went to America–I had met Tom and Bert earlier–they were very prepared to be friendly, and so was I. Like us, Tom and Jeannie had not been married very long. We all got on well and would go out every week for meals and spend lots of time together off the course. Bert and Linda already had children, so Linda was only occasionally out on tour. But between tournaments we might stay at their house for the odd week.

'I very much enjoyed playing golf with Tom and Bert–the greatest help to me was just watching them swing the golf club, because I was always a good mimic as a boy and learned my golf from mimicry as most children do. I found it very beneficial to be around them. I can close my eyes now and see Tom's swing, and it's a good thing to have that picture as he has the classic golf swing. His mentor was Tommy Bolt with whom I played a lot of golf and soon realised it was passed from Tommy to Tom.

'Tom's personality was difficult, whereas now it's much better because he's a lot more mature than he was. I remember playing with him in a practice round at Birkdale when we were taking yardages, and Tom had sliced his tee shot at the 10th. He was moaning at us: "you guys aren't helping me to look for my ball." I said jokingly, oh you poor old sod, why don't you clear off. Then he sulked. Later he came up to me and said, "Oh I'm sorry TJ" (he always called me that). We had a good relationship.

'One time when we were all staying with Yancey, Tom missed the cut having played like an idiot. He came back to the house and went to bed for two days and wouldn't come out of his room. The fact was, he knew he was like that, and when he came out he knew he was ready to emerge, which was fine. I never saw anything wrong in that. He does what he feels is right and you can't knock it.

'He would probably have had better results had he been a bit more mature when he was younger. Because of his anger over the silly things he did, the accumulation of it all was that he would shut off his mind and therefore he stopped learning. Rather than analysing what happened – it was his anger that took over and his mind went blank. In fact, all that he got angry about was the fact that he wasn't perfect on the golf course.

'He did realise his potential and proved what he could do in 1973 when he had a fantastic year, winning the Open Championship, four tournaments in America, one in South Africa, the World Series of Golf, and nearly $250,000 in prize-money. The thing that motivated him was his father's death in the early part of the year and he dug down deep to some lower regions of his mind and produced the golf of which he was capable.

'Whatever potential you have, you still have to give 100 per cent. To dig deep, you've got to really concentrate and drive yourself. The majority cannot drive themselves that hard. Everyone has periods in life when they play very well, but they are highly concentrated and they're giving up a terrific amount to do it. Subconsciously, maybe one is not prepared to feel that way all the time. Tom probably wasn't.

'Whatever you win it's always the same feeling: you're bloody nervous but your mind has to be controlled – it's very much a total self-control situation. That's a very difficult area.

'To a great extent Tom is in a similar situation to mine, with respect to the fact that secretly everyone really expected him to do a lot better than he's done, although he has done exceptionally well. At the end of it, you have to come to terms with yourself and not all the other hamburgers.

'Bert had a quite different personality. He was very quiet. We used to call him "the fog" because he would walk around in a land of his own and forget things. He would sometimes walk off the course and then just disappear without saying anything – he was a real loner.

'I was quite close to Bert, I really liked him. I found him very intelligent and he was also a mystery. I roomed with Bert once or twice and we could sit and not say anything for ages, which suited me. We had a lot of fun.

'The trouble was that he had a problem and the last thing you want to be doing when you have any sort of mental problem is to be playing golf. He worked hard at his game but he just happened to have a chemical deficiency which sent him over the top and he went berserk in public.

'Things do happen in this world like Bert's falling apart, and it takes a hell of a lot to surprise me now. I know that sounds blasé, but first I was mildly surprised and then I was very sorry. I find it very embarrassing – I'm embarrassed for him. He must feel awful now he's quite all right.

'Just imagine how I would feel if I went berserk, did something stupid, and it was in all the papers all over the land and everyone knew. They put you away for a while until you're all right and then you've got to go out and face these people again. I feel uncomfortable for him.

'When I saw him after his breakdown I tried to be the same as I was before, not to do any more than that as I wanted him to feel as normal as possible. I acted the same because I have a feeling for the guy. If someone makes a fool of themselves on a stage you feel terrible for them and say, let me out, I've got to go, it's not a nice situation. Bert's in that situation, not from his own doing but because he became ill. On the whole people are very good, but it must be very embarrassing for him and I don't want to show pity or he'll feel it's not the same as it was before.

'Of course it isn't the same. Bert and Linda are now divorced. They had four children and I knew them all and spent many happy times with them at their two homes, fishing, swimming, eating lobsters–and those fantastic times are all ended. It's very sad but life goes on. We, the Yanceys and the Weiskopfs have all grown apart. Everyone's life has changed.'

TOM AND JEAN WEISKOPF

Tom and Jean Weiskopf are both genuinely fond of Tony and Vivien Jacklin. They talk of them and their friendship in warm terms. During the 1978 Open Championship at St Andrews they took time to talk about Tony, his family, and his problems as they've known them over the years.

Tom Weiskopf

'I've known Tony Jacklin and his family since 1968. I was introduced to Tony through Bert Yancey, who was a close friend of mine. Then the three of us became very close friends and I think we still are, but we don't see much of each other for a lot of reasons. We have families, we're older, we have different responsibilities, and our positions on the Tour are different.

'Tony once played the US Tour on a week to week basis. Then he won the two Opens in the space of a year and his life changed. Then fortunately I won a few tournaments and my life changed. If you become successful in golf your time is taken up with other things. It's no longer the Mondays, Tuesdays and Wednesdays that were Bert Yancey, Tony Jacklin and Tom Weiskopf days–they may not end but they are cut back quite a bit. At the time, golf was the most important thing for us to do, and we practised, played and gambled on our golf together.

'Tony became much more successful than either Bert or I did. I won my first major in 1973, but when Tony won his he became a national hero. If I won my national Open I would not be a national hero because the United States is such an enormous place and there are so many heroes. There's a week to week response and appreciation shown towards winners but to be a hero you'd have to be a continual winner of the major championships. You can't compare the countries. Britain is small, there aren't many people and what Tony Jacklin achieved in a year, no one else has ever done. It was a spark in the life of British golf and boosted it.

'After Tony won, he never changed to me as a person. I saw the same qualities. He always had time for me, and he still does. He treats everyone equally. He was a very fair player to play with, he didn't moan or complain. He was and always has been a gentleman.

'He's had bitter disappointments–we all have–but he always kept his sense of humour. I think that's the greatest quality that Tony Jacklin has. I saw him once when it looked like he was going to burst into tears, right after Lee Trevino did that inexplicable thing to Tony in the 1972 Open at Muirfield. When I saw him as he came off the course, I had nothing to say to him because I understood what he was going through. Then he said something that made us both laugh. I can't remember it, but it was at a time when it looked like he was going to cry.

'Tony may lose his patience at times with people, maybe he doesn't sign every autograph he should and he may not do what others expect of him all the time. Because of what he did, he put himself in a different position from any other player in the modern era of British golf. Tony Jacklin is a good ambassador. I've seen him in the United States and he never loses his cool. He knows how to control his temperament, how to hide his emotions. Those are qualities that I look for in friendship. Most of my friends are like that–very different from myself–I'm moody, unpredictable, an up and down type of person, especially when I'm playing golf. Tony seems to go on one level and Bert Yancey is an easy going guy. I think they are average people. Tony likes fish and chips and the down-to-earth things of life, although his success may have made it difficult for him to live like that.

'I have a so-called temper but I don't think I'm different from anyone else, it's just that outwardly I express myself more than others with my moods. I'm spontaneous and I don't plan things, they just happen and I don't know why. The Press has always tried to build me up as the next superstar, so when their instant hero doesn't do all the things he is supposed to do, there has to be a reason. I've never given a golf club the helicopter treatment. I've thrown it down at my bag but I've never been fined for throwing a club, or for profanity. I would get so upset with myself that I would walk off the golf course, which I've done only five times in 13 years. Other guys do it five times in a year.

'But when you're up there on a pedestal, there's got to be a reason for everything. They dubbed me temperamental and they say that's the reason why I didn't become a superstar. But I'm happier than all of them and so is Tony Jacklin, because he's got a super wife who has never changed, I call her Lady Jacklin, and who cares about all the money that you make? He's got nice friends and great children who are well behaved.

'We have all matured. Bert Yancey had a nice wife and four great kids, but it just didn't all work out. He had problems that I didn't realise or foresee and it was very upsetting when I was playing with him in 1975 at Westchester and he cracked up. We were paired together the first two days and Bert was very irrational. I was really worried because he was talking in a funny way, had a wild look in his eyes and probably it would not have hurt me to stay out there, but I didn't want to see my best friend have a nervous breakdown on the golf course, and I walked in with the crowd heckling him still having five holes to play. I was asked why by the PGA, and I said it was for personal reasons. They fined me $3,000. Yancey finished his round and that night he had a breakdown at the airport.

'I was quickly criticised by the Press. I had been fined more than anyone had ever been fined for walking off the course. I didn't tell anyone what it was all about, but a year and a half later Bert asked me about it, and he told everyone.

'I judge Bert and Tony on the time that I'm with them, on how they treat me and what they've been to me—helpful at times, courteous and understanding. Hearsay doesn't mean a damned thing to me—what people think and say. I would fight for them because they are friends.

'With hindsight, which is always easier, I would like to have seen Tony move to the United States for 10 years, though I realise that customs and the language to a certain extent are different, and it would have been difficult. But he would have been exempt and playing our Tour full-time, which was where he had changed and improved his golf game from 1968 onwards, and then by coming back to Britain he had to change it again to play in the different conditions.

'The weather can be terrible in Britain. It doesn't give you a chance to play golf on certain days because you have to put on so many sweaters. You can't swing, you're just slapping the ball at times, not playing golf. We play in wind in America, but usually we play in 90-degree heat and wear shirts. Added to that, the British courses are of the type that make you play defensive golf, unlike those in the United States.

'Tony made the decision to come back to Europe and he was paid appearance money which was fair and it was great—I think I would have accepted the same type of deal. But then he didn't perform to their standards and he gave people a reason to criticise, because he was being paid for his performance. They said, he's spoiled, he doesn't care because he gets a few thousand pounds to play. But they paid him because he gave British golf a shot in the arm.

'Not performing well hurt Tony's pride just as much as it hurt the sponsors who were dishing out the money when he missed the cut. In fact it hurt his pride more than their pocket books. Now they slap him in the face. But they created the problem, it was they who came to him, he didn't go to them—that's what people forget—he merely accepted their offer.

'Then Tony tried going back to America to play and he's got to make another whole transformation in his game. On top of that, he's a double Open champion and people just don't follow him, which hurts his pride. So now he's really confused.

'We didn't discuss it because he never broached the subject, and I don't volunteer information to my friends unless they ask for advice as I wouldn't want to hurt their feelings. It's their privacy and the thing we

94

honour with each other. We don't intrude into each other's feelings.

'I do think the Press in Britain is one of the strongest there is–they are so critical, it's unbelievable. Tony perhaps left himself open to criticism but there's a lack of compassion in the writing in Britain. It's almost as though they know their players are going to lose, or their team, even before they get involved in the thing. We knew they were going to get beaten, they say. They are factual, they're strongly opinionated and they tend to crush people down rather than build them up. I love the descriptive writing, it's fantastic, but the Americans project the feelings of the players and sympathise a bit more.

'Tony's never been a quitter–that guy is a competitor. If he weren't he wouldn't have achieved what he has. Of course people want to build up their heroes and knock them down. You know why that is? It's envy. Because they didn't do it there's a lot of envy.

'I envy a lot of people because they can do things better than I can, but I wouldn't knock them. I'm a bit envious of Jack Nicklaus–he's done some things that are just incredible–but it's an enviable respect. I'd never admit to Nicklaus that I wish I'd won five Masters and I haven't won one: I've been runner-up four times. I've had the chances but Nicklaus has been able to do something to which I've come very close, but I can't do it. It's a very frustrating thing. To me, to win certain tournaments and perform well is important, but a super wife, and two super kids are just great for me, and when people remark on them, that's a reward.

'I've done exactly what I wanted to do in my life so far. If Tony and I had sacrificed a bit more, maybe we both would have won many more tournaments. There will be a time when I can't play any more and I will wish I had done more. Tony and I can do just what we want to do and maybe we are too much of the prima donna at times. At least Tony Jacklin won the two greatest championships that there are in golf–they can never rub his name off the cups.

'Maybe at one time he decided he wanted to be the world's greatest player and then something happened. Maybe it's just too much to beat balls every day like a Ben Hogan who devoted his life to golf, he never even had a guest room in his house.

'My best golf year in 1973 was the worst with my wife and family. There were two babies, and I never saw my wife for four months and she was travelling with me. I was so involved with golf, with commercials and business that I once didn't eat dinner with her for eight straight days. I said, to hell with that; if that's what it takes to be the greatest golfer in the world, I don't want it.

'Maybe Tony decided against all that running around. You continually change your lifestyle, your outlook and you mellow, your goals change. Obviously Tony changed from being aggressive, tenacious and dedicated. The pressure of travelling all over the world got to him, and being away from his family. When he wasn't recognised in America, he thought why beat my head against a wall, why not try to win and enjoy myself at home?

'I feel sorry for Tony in respect of the fact that he doesn't win more, because I know that he should–not five or six times a year but once or twice a year. He was always a hard guy to beat once he got ahead of you. As a golfer there was nothing that over-impressed me about the mechanical side of his game. He was a bit inconsistent which is fine–a lot of players are like that. He had a sharp mind, knew how to manage himself and difficult courses, and I can't think of another British player that's had the guts of Tony Jacklin. This guy had guts.'

Jean Weiskopf

'Our friendship with Tony and Vivien is one that we can all pick up where we left off–it's not some people we used to know very well–ours was a real friendship. Certainly golf started it, but we had a lot of similar thoughts about things. For instance, Vivien and I view wifely jobs in the same way. We both spoil our men and a lot of women don't. We go through out little "Women's Lib" feelings every now and then, like: "I am a person too" but really we're not radical "Libbers".

'The guys both love their golf and they love their families. Tony may be regretting giving up the United States, but he is very happy that he can be with his family. I think the British people are upset because they wanted him to go on and be the best in the world. There's only one Nicklaus and one Player, men who can give their whole life to a sport.

'It's not a bad thing to fall back on your family. My first year of staying home without Tom when our first child was in school was awful. I cried, I was depressed and lonely. I didn't want Tom to know and say, all right, I'll come home–I just wanted to be with him. Vivien says she felt the same. Tom would be gone three weeks but at least he was in the United States, and I could, if I needed to, get on a 'plane and see him for the weekend. Vivien couldn't when Tony was in America, which makes it harder.

'Sometimes Tony gets a little defensive, but he's had to be like that because someone is always saying, why did you do that, or what's the matter with your golf? It's like saying to a woman, what's the matter with your hair? Do you really want to look like that? If her hair is really ugly, of course she doesn't. Equally, Tony wants to play or putt better–he's a winner, he's not trying to lose. But the constant pressure makes him defensive and he becomes too emphatic.

'They all suffer a lot. Anyone out there who is really good goes through hell sometimes because his game can disappear, fall out from under him. But it does come back. If Tom gets in a slump the Press talk about it a little, but there are so many other heroes. There have been times though when Tom has been upset with the publicity. When he was told he should continue to win five out of eight tournaments as he did in 1973–well nobody does that, and how he ever did it is unbelievable. To say he should have maintained that peak of brilliance is not realistic. But they tried to say, why aren't you doing it all the time? The answer is, because it's not possible, that's why. However, Tom began to think, I'm just a big jerk, I can't play golf any more–which was nonsense.

'In Tony's case they didn't have anyone else on whom to focus. They tried to make Peter Oosterhuis into something to take over where Tony left off, but it never happened. It's still really on Tony and that's a big burden to carry. The more you force it the worse it is, and the guys get into that vicious cycle. About 75 per cent of the game is mental. You can go to the practice tee and see so many good golf swings and good putting strokes, but who can make it happen when he wants to? Maybe Jack Nicklaus can but not very many. In golf, occasionally someone has a brilliant week and then it may not happen again until next year.

'Nicklaus does it all the time–and he's special. To be able to turn it on when you want to excites me. There's nothing personal about it, I just think it's so exciting to know there is someone who can turn it on when he has to. It's freaky genius, like an Einstein who can figure out things the other man couldn't begin to conceive.

'Tony was very popular in the United States. Americans are always pleased to see someone new come along, and they just love winners. Winning is part of the American way of life–it's a real positive country. On the Tour, there could have been some golfers who resented his winning, because there are golfers on Tour who resent anyone winning. Maybe in the locker-room they weren't patting him on the back as much as they do in Britain but I don't think the public left him with negative feelings.

'Tom is very honest, never a hypocrite, so is Tony, and it can hurt them. When suddenly Tony was disillusioned with America, he said, I don't want to be over here. Then certain people reacted and said, who do you think you are? We're Americans, this is the greatest country in the world.

'Tony is a perfectionist and he expects as much from other people, which is one reason why he and Vivien do so well together–she's the same way. They are both very giving people and they demand something as well. They want to do whatever they do in the best way, maybe not the best of anybody, but the best they can do it, which is a perfect attitude. You don't have to beat everyone else but you can always try to do your best.

'Certain women are much better geared to being married to professional golfers. There's a real type. The girls are competitive, assertive, and they tend to desire perfection a little more.

'Tony and Vivien are happy. They are pleased they moved to Jersey. When everything is over and he is 50–and very few guys are out playing golf then–he and Vivien are still going to have their nice little family that they enjoy so much. He certainly doesn't have to win golf tournaments to pay the bills and he's going to have a very nice life. Even though the British won't be able to say he was the greatest golfer in the world he was very good for them for a while and he still has a lot of talent.'

12: Gentlemen of the Press

TONY'S RELATIONSHIP with the Press, with the regular golf writers on the Tour, has been an essentially happy one. On occasions there have been feelings of animosity, usually as the result of frustration and disappointment on both sides.

Tony was asked about his performances – good and bad – because he was, and still is, the only British golfer with whom people identify and care about passionately. He talked freely about his golf, indulging, in the Press tent, in the kind of therapy that every golfer needs after a good or bad round of golf – there's the compulsion to tell someone about it.

For the Press it was a delightful epoch to have a hero who looked good, talked well and played some magical golf. Then it was upsetting to have him fall from the top in such bewildering fashion. Although it may have caused a few to make some disparaging comments, there still remains among the Press an enormous regard for Tony, both as a person and for what he has achieved. They are as captivated as the public by his personality and, in addition, the Press acknowledge the difference he has made to their lives.

Latterly Tony has developed feelings of resentment about the Press and his image. 'Why is it that Arnold Palmer has never had bad Press in all the years he has played?' demands Tony. 'You get the feeling the Press would be lynched for writing anything bad about him.' But Arnold Palmer is a genius at public relations, and a very tactful man.

Michael McDonnell is the golf writer for the *Daily Mail* and comments thus: 'First of all you have to remember the nature of newspapers in this country. We are a nation of readers. There are massive circulations and because of those factors we are the only nation in the world that has so many full-time golf reporters, cricket reporters or soccer reporters, due to the massive interest. The fact that we are in business, doing the job we are, is a reflection of that national reading habit.

'In the case of Jacklin, he became a national figure; not just a good sportsman, not just a handy golfer – a Bernard Hunt or Brian Huggett – he became national in the same way as Henry Cooper, Terry Downes, Denis Compton or Henry Cotton. These people transcended their sport. At that status, you are film star level and everything happens.

'Jacklin was not just on the sports pages – he was on the front page, in gossip columns, everywhere. It's something he couldn't reconcile himself to accepting, that there was this public curiosity. It is a problem that any public personality of that magnitude has to face and come to terms with it. There was the good side. The enormous spreads that Jacklin got about moving house were a plus, and against those, anything else, if it was mildly critical, was regarded as bad publicity.

'At the same time, he set himself phenomenal standards by winning the two major championships in the space of 12 months. Unfairly perhaps, he is then going to be judged by that standard thereafter. I don't think anyone other than Nicklaus could maintain that standard, but neither do I think Jacklin should have declined the way he did.

'I could hazard a guess at his decline and say in golf there have been a lot of one-time winners, and he was really a one-time winner and the fact that he won twice was part of a magnificent piece of good fortune. He could have won three more Opens, but he didn't. He should have won at Muirfield, but he didn't. Speculating, you may well find that 1972 and Muirfield undermined his confidence.

'A good golfer once told me that there are beatings and there are bad beatings. With a bad beating you actually question your own ability, your own worth–you have real doubts about your value. Both at the Muirfield Open and in the Piccadilly World Match-Play when he shot 63 in the afternoon, Jacklin had played the best golf of his life and he lost.

'I also think that people know when they're going to win. They won't tell us–Gary Player does now and again–but they have some kind of conviction, not just a belief or hope–they know. I think Jacklin expected his name to be on the trophy at Muirfield and when Trevino beat him, his confidence was shattered. There is a lack of something in Jacklin, what it is I don't know. All great golfers inevitably find themselves getting involved in horrendous defeats. But he should never have lost that Open, yet he did, he let someone beat him. It's your status that is involved and the fact you've failed in this manner can be damaging.

'The process of winning puts you through a psychological mangle. The strains and tensions are such that it can be unbearable. Tony knows what it's like, knows what is involved, he's been there and now he doesn't want to go through it again. He'll deny it, say of course I want it. But something won't let him go through it.

'Look at his qualifications. Here's a man who should now be in the prime of his competitive life. You will not find anybody who doesn't say that he hits the ball as well, if not better, than at any time in his life. He's fit, has no money worries, and he says it's just the putting. It's not just the putting. The attitude towards putting, the motivation is perhaps part and parcel of what I'm talking about. They used to say Palmer willed it into the hole; "we may be 25 feet from the hole, but you are going in," he would say–I think that's gone with Jacklin.

'It's nothing to do with money and if he were skint now he still couldn't do it. He would play a much tighter game but it wouldn't make him any more of a winner. He hasn't lost the desire to win, he's lost the stomach and the compulsion to win. There's no way a man who did as much as he did, could fade the way he has done. Even his most loyal supporters are now beginning to question whether this is just an inevitable trough that all golfers go through. We're talking now about a Jacklin who doesn't even contend in tournaments. We're not talking about winning Open Championships or tournaments, but about a man who is not challenging in week to week events. That's how sad things have become.

'I didn't think Jacklin would tail off. I thought there was nothing to stop him, he was supremely confident, he always had a great zest for the good things and the sky was the limit. I thought he would go on because there was nothing to stop him. Look at him now. He swings it beautifully, he's fit and strong–why isn't he doing it? You have to start probing, coming up with theories and speculation about what has gone wrong and whether it can be put right.

'Until 1973 he loved all the attention, it was no bother. You could get Tony Jacklin's telephone number easily, even when it went ex-directory– he was always available. Recently he has gone through a period where no one has the 'phone number. He said, you blighters aren't getting it and someone replied, we don't need it Tony. I'm told he didn't have the number put on the telephones so that anyone who came in couldn't look and take it–they didn't even tell his son, Bradley, what it was. If you wanted to get in touch with Jacklin, you telephoned Tommy Horton in Jersey, who acted as an exchange. He 'phoned Jacklin, who would then ring you. He hasn't been plagued or pestered by the Press over the last few years; maybe a few snide remarks, but not interviews in the home, pictures in the lounge and that sort of thing. Yet the speed with which he 'phones you back once the message has got through suggests that he is quite happy to talk, and when you get him he is very good. But there's a great danger of him becoming a bit of a sad figure, and I feel sorry.

'Jacklin wasn't a great golfer–he was very good. Peter Thomson said to me in 1969 at Lytham: "He's good, but he's not yet great" and that was a champion passing his judgement on someone who had just won the title. Only time can prove greatness and you have to win a lot of times.

'People say he had that magnificent year. Some people call it the magnificent fortnight–just two weeks when everything went right for him and nothing since.

'You can start by analysing what he did against Tom Watson off the 18th tee in the final round at Pebble Beach in the 1977 Bing Crosby tournament. The old Jacklin would have drilled the ball straight up there the way he drilled the ball down the last hole at Lytham, with no fear at all, fully aware he was going to win, that was his appointment and his name was going on the trophy. When he played in the Crosby he was aware of what could go wrong. That old arrogance and conceit, in a nice way, that every good golfer must have had gone.

'Now it may well be maturity. The older we get, the more we realise our limitations. But that didn't stop Player or Nicklaus, although they are phenomenal and should be excluded from discussion. Player is fanatical and Nicklaus must be, or he wouldn't do what he is doing. At the moment Jacklin is in the Weiskopf category. He has not yet done enough to become a great player and time is running out. I'd like to see Jacklin come back, but as time goes on the fact that he doesn't suggests that he won't and more than won't – can't.

'Certainly the British Press is desperate for idols. As soon as there is one the Press build him up, then look round for the slightest sign of weakness. Jacklin doesn't keep enough back. He has been badly advised in terms of never having anyone who had his image at heart. No one said, this is the wise thing to do for your image, this is good public relations.

'Also, so many times there was an apparent lack of judgment. I'm going to America, he said, that's where my future is; then no, I want to come back and be with my family. I'll buy the baronial hall in Gloucestershire; no, this is too much, I'll move to Jersey. Perhaps it is the nature of the man, the headstrong, independent streak that made him a champion, that also led him to make these kind of mistakes and the two things are inseparable.

'But there should have been some sort of advice, a father figure in his life to advise him – I don't think his own father had that sort of influence on him. Someone like Tony doesn't give his respect to people very easily. I bet that he doesn't really truly respect many people. He might respect Jack Nicklaus's performance, his stamina as a champion. But because Jacklin had such a good rapport with the Press, because he was such a good talker – he felt he could handle it all himself, anyway. It would be very hard to advise him.

'The curious thing about Jacklin is that he is still a charismatic figure. If you go round golf clubs now, people want to know what's wrong with Jacklin, they don't want to know about Peter Oosterhuis or Nick Faldo. It's a backhanded measure of your importance that even when you're doing badly you're the centre of attention. Everyone will follow him when he's playing – it's the charisma, the star quality.

'We so-called cynical knockers, the journalists, all want him to do well, we're still putting bets on him. Certainly he improved my lot, my standard of living. What he did for golf by broadening the horizons gave us all spin-offs. He epitomised the new wave in golf and everyone owes him a lot indirectly and directly in some cases. I've always acknowledged that and I think all the Press would. But it's not gratitude that makes us want him to do well, it's something about the man. It's a phenomenon I don't understand.

'You know if he did win, he'd be back to his old arrogance, impatient and full of himself. You'd put up with it because you want him to do well. That doesn't apply to any other figure. Henry Cooper and Graham Hill are probably the only two other sportsmen who got close to that kind of warmth. Jacklin hasn't cultivated it – it's just something that happened.

It's personality, star appeal, some have it, others don't. That is why he remains in demand years after he has won a tournament of any note.'

Peter Ryde, golf writer for *The Times*: 'I think the Press gave Tony cause for complaint. I've always blamed the Press to a very large extent because I think they pursued him whatever happened and expected him to give them a story after he'd done a 74 or 75, when there simply wasn't a story there.

'But Tony was always willing to talk, which I think was due to his grounding in America where he learned the art of talking to the Press. He had to as they are generally far more articulate than our professionals, and he learned that and came back and used it with good effect when he was winning. But when he went through the bad times he was still pursued by the Press, not hounded, but asked for a quote, just to say something even after a poor round. The result of that was inevitable. What can you say about a round of 74 if you have to say something? You must give a reason why it wasn't less and therefore you sound in the end as though you're making excuses however smart you are at talking.

'I honestly think – and I don't like lumping together the Press as one, but it's the safest way to do it – that they are really quite responsible for making Tony look a loudmouth, someone who was always finding excuses for his game, and I don't believe that is his nature.

'The end effect is that a large part of his troubles arose from over-exposure, and a lot of that came from having to talk about himself on the days when he wasn't going well. He always met the Press and gave out – that's his nature. In the end, when his confidence began to go and he became more and more aware of himself, and it was harder to get it all back, the exposure embarrassed him.

'The excuse for the Press is that the public are hero worshippers always looking for a hero. The Press is trying to find a hero for them and it also makes it easier for them to write so they build up the hero figure and keep him in the picture as long as possible. I know that is the attitude in most newspapers – and it's not an unreasonable one – that you concentrate on the big names. If you're writing about tennis, the Sports Editors say follow Nastase, he's a story. If it's golf, certainly Tony was the only one at the top to write about, that's what the Sports Editors wanted and to that extent the writers were only doing their job. But I'm sure it had an adverse effect on Tony.

'I think he created his putting problem by talking about his bad rounds. Inevitably you say, if only I had got in four six-footers – I would have had a good round. If you read that often enough, you become affected by it. But you can't expect the Press to consider a player's feelings to that extent. The newspaper's duty is to its readers and however fond the writer may be of the individual, his duty is to the paper.

'Tony could have said, get off my back – how the hell can I talk about a

Newspaper cuttings showing the treatment given to Tony's successes.

round of 74. He's got enough charm to get away with it, if he had chosen to do that. He could have done it without offending the golf writers.

'Neither did I think it helped his image a bit, when after the interviews on the golf, he would talk about his cars, his moustache, or things like that. To a certain extent it's one of the hazards of the job and you become conscious of your own image. But interview rooms can be dangerous places, and the fact that he was the only hero, doing it all, didn't help.

'Initially I expected him to have a longer career. Then I could see that he was having so much taken out of him and it was really all on his shoulders – all the fame, the credit, the blame – it was obviously going to wear him out. The whole thing depends on how much you give out, what it takes out of you and how long you can go on. Arnold Palmer burned himself out long before Gary Player, very much due to the fact of what he gave out. Jack Nicklaus takes less out of himself because he is less involved emotionally.

'Then Tony tried to bestride the Atlantic and no one has ever done that. Great players come over here and win the Open Championship – but to run lives on both sides at once has never been achieved. Probably though, when Tony started, you had to go to America to prove yourself. He was the one who built up the British circuit more than any other single man – he got the prize-money increased through his achievements. Before that, it was so small you had to go to America – in the same way that Gary Player had to come out of South Africa.

103

'You don't need to be sophisticated to settle down to living in America. Rather the reverse in fact–the simpler your approach, the easier it is to get on. Coming from a small town background you can settle there, but you can't do both, that is live here and play there. Tony tried to do both because he loves his home over here and did not want to live in America.

'When I think of Tony Jacklin when I first saw him as a boy, it was as an international at Dalmahoy in 1961, I can't remember anything, except this extraordinary zest and the way he went up the fairway. He had that certain something, the attack, the thrust that you might have used on the stage, like Laurence Olivier or like Nicklaus taking charge of a golf course–he takes it over. It's an inner confidence that radiates and when you come up against it you can recognise it, it's innate. You could almost feel it then. Tony was a born winner, that was the quality shining out. He's just the successful type.

'He was ambitious but I doubt that he knew what for, that he had any clear idea of lifestyle when he was winning the big ones. I remember once when he went off and bought another Rolls-Royce, Mark McCormack said, "that's Tony, you can't do anything about it–he does things on impulse off the top of his head." Which suggests that he never had any calculated ideas about lifestyle.

'Obviously at some point when you've done it, achieved what you want, the fire goes out in the boiler. His bad luck was to win those two big ones close together. Had they been spread out over say four years, success would have been so much easier to take. The heights that he scaled would have been gradual instead of shooting straight to the top within a year. It was much harder to handle and I think he took it awfully well.

'He did suffer a lot from the attention of the Press. It was almost as though the Press had a guilt complex for not giving him his due when he was doing the great things–he got hardly any coverage for his US Open win as there were only three journalists out there.

'But Tony was too susceptible to what was written about him, he was not tough enough with the British Press. It was not a question of coming up against them, it was just a matter of being tactful, not so forthcoming and willing to talk. Palmer was more subtle in his handling of the Press, he was very exceptional–a past master at it. He can take the most stupid question in the world, turn it slightly and make the man think he's asked a pretty good question. Palmer took more out of himself than Nicklaus, who has his own way of handling the Press which is very effective–he'd snub the fellow quite pleasantly, there'd be a laugh and that would be that. Sometimes with Jacklin, it would seem as though you'd uncorked a bottle and it all had to come out. He was largely responsible in that it wasn't a matter of squeezing it out, and to that extent it could have been avoided on his part.

'Now I see Tony going on as he is, making a very good living. I see him winning the occasional smaller event, not a big one. He's the best swinger

*Putting agonies are no
strangers to Arnold Palmer
or Tony.*

of a golf club in Britain since the war, but he's used up his reserves for the big ones. He has dug pretty deep. But we haven't written that, so he can't blame the Press for giving him that label.'

Ben Wright, golf writer for the *Financial Times* and CBS television golf commentator in America: 'I've been going to America since 1966 and I've had a very happy alliance with Tony. The highspot of that time was being at the US Open at Chaska, when he won.

'I enjoyed Tony's company when I was there, but he didn't make friends easily amongst the players in the States. Weiskopf and Yancey were his two big buddies and they were rather outsiders themselves, so it was somewhat like three outsiders together. Weiskopf is a little funny in the head and Yancey has gone funny. Weiskopf has never been popular with his brother professionals because they think he's a nut. The three guys got on well together, possibly because they were forced into these circumstances, or maybe they were a bit alike.

'I've a great deal of time for Tom, but he is a Jekyll and Hyde personality. He and Yancey both looked after Tony, as you would a nephew, when he first arrived on the Tour. Tony was a lonely boy – if he hadn't been, he would like to have got by without them.

'At first it was all marvellous for Tony in America and they were impressed by how hard he worked when he arrived. Then there was a decline in his work rate – success went to his head. He thought he could still do it with half the work and he started to hang around the clubhouse instead of the practice tee. There was a time when he was going through the motions out there and expecting to still keep winning. When it didn't happen, it was almost a personal insult.

'He began saying bad things about the US Tour and they won't forgive you for that when you have enjoyed the fruits. While you've got them behind you, you're fine but if they turn against you they can be very vicious. I saw it all happening and I dreaded it at the time. Sometimes I wanted to get him by the scruff of the neck and shake him because I liked him so much and do still.

'I was terribly disappointed because he had the world at his feet and he chose to kick it away. I have remained very loyal to Tony and I have almost never written a bad word about him. Let's face it – I was riding on Tony's coat-tails. Hell, it hasn't hurt me having knocked around with Jacklin in the good old days – it's not done my career any harm. So I felt a great personal involvement. I've always felt so much more warmth towards Jacklin than I could feel for any other player. He had that charisma which caught me up like a fan. I was far less impartial than I might have been, which was wrong, but it was something I couldn't help – he was a magical guy.

'I went overboard on him back in 1965 because I reckoned I could see what he was going to be. I arranged to interview him at the Sunningdale Foursomes that year, where he was playing with Alex Caygill and he was nothing, a nobody. He was just a kid, and he turned up for the interview –I'll never forget–in gold lamé pants, gold cashmere sweater over a white polo neck, and gold shoes. I thought, well that's great–this kid really believes in himself.

'It was my first ever meeting with him and I was wild about him. I thought he had presence, he had the talent, the work rate, and I loved him for it. It was manna from heaven. I had been writing about the game since 1954, and I said here's a kid who has really got it.

'I was always a great champion of Jacklin. He came out as a rather brash young man–and he was–but he believed in himself and realised he had to do the work. No one worked any harder at the game than he did in those formative years.

'I don't think Tony was well guided, nor did he learn some of the lessons he might have along the way–such as being discreet. Maybe this brashness made him what he was, I don't know. Of late, he has said a lot of stupid things, which as a hero I would rather he had not said. You always want your heroes to do everything right and I don't think he has verbally.

'Of course his grossest error of all was his house at Winchcombe. Setting up as a Cotswold landowner in the midst of very difficult, snobbish people was the wrong thing. He didn't fit in. Elsham in Lincolnshire was such a fantastic place, all his buddies were there, and you can get to London Airport from there–you just have to start a bit earlier. It was a stupid mistake and it was then he started to lose it all.

'Now, I don't think he'll ever win another Open. Goodness knows I'd love to see it. But to go on failing is the worst thing mentally in golf, and in my experience if you let it slip as far as he has, you never get it back again unless you're a fellow like Ben Hogan, to whom golf is all of life. It isn't to Tony and never has been.

'It's totally understandable that a kid who did a newspaper round, who knew what it was like to be poor, would find it difficult to be told how to go about things when he became rich.

'When you know a kid has had no formal education, you know he's coming up in a big way and what happens to people like that–boxers and so on, who are not the most intelligent people in the world, they're unable to cope with it all–and managers ought to do more to look after this aspect. They are there to do things like that.

'A few people in the Press may have been a bit savage with him at times. But if you get yourself in his position, you've got to take that. It's no good bitching about it. Tony gets desperately offended, he is very sensitive to criticism, instead of realising they've got the power to do it and shrugging it off. When he is on top, everything is fine. When he slips a little, he is shown in his true light.'

Peter Dobereiner, golf writer for *The Observer*: 'When Jacklin won his two Open Championships he was always the biggest news, the Press had to write about him. Golf being a game where even when you are the greatest, you only produce marvellous rounds and some marvellous tournaments three or four times a year, perforce it had to be: "Jacklin fails", because this is the nature of the game. Jacklin reacted against that. The fellows wanted to go on writing that he won, but he didn't, and for a long time the fact that he hadn't won was bigger news than the winner.

'There is not a man in the Press tent who doesn't want him to win. The snide element you get in the writing reflects the frustration for Jacklin of the writer, and of course Jacklin feels this frustration 100 times more. It's hard not being able to write about him as the superstar. It was much easier when he was at the top. It was marvellous for the Press, we all felt better, very happy for him and now he has let us down a bit in that sense – simply because we relate to him. The vindictive writing comes from the gossip writers. The public see him as a standard bearer who failed them.

'Jacklin built himself up through his career, he wasn't manufactured. He was a nice young kid with a lot of ambition and drive, and a good golf game. The thing that made him a champion was this dream of the big house, the Rolls-Royce, the beautiful wife and kids, and the country squire. Then he got all that and found it didn't really mean very much to him. He couldn't keep it because of tax and that is what soured him – the impetus that had been driving him on to his goal was gone. Once he achieved it he found it was hollow. He enjoyed it only for about six months, and he couldn't hang on to it or play golf at that time. He needed a new stimulus and since then all the stimuli have been negative for him – trying to get back up to where he was, which is very different from going up there the first time.

'Jacklin never had the ambition just to win tournaments, as strongly as Jack Nicklaus, Tom Watson or Henry Cotton. He was never driven by this obsession to prove himself to be the greatest golfer. He wanted to be the richest golfer and that was part of the trouble. Now he chooses lucrative events, he goes for the easy money. It's a fairly subtle but clear distinction. I don't think Nicklaus has thought about money since the day he turned professional, that is from the point of view of an objective. There are plenty of poor people who have the same drive to become the greatest golfer – they may not succeed – but it's got to be that way round to be an enduring champion. Jacklin's booster rocket fizzled out when he got there. Now he's got to try to re-motivate himself which is very difficult.

'He got very brassed off with some of the Press attention. But life, or golf, is all about being able to shrug it off and get on with it, in spite of all the distractions. He never took any great satisfaction in his good Press notices and I don't think it bothers him when people are a bit snide.

'He got the reputation for being a moaner because we wanted him to go on being a champion and we always asked him why, why, why? He always said something different, mainly because he was being grilled and he said far too much.

'The last thing he can afford to do now is to admit that he's not such a good player after all. Therefore, as self-defence he has to cast round for reasons for his higher scores. We go through the unfortunate charade of putting, income tax, property tax; he couldn't combine golf and travel, he didn't like the food, he was homesick for his wife and kids. We've had a succession of these excuses, some more plausible than others—none of them very valid. The fact is, he's not played as well as he did. It's as simple as that. Sure he had it in him to do it, but when it went wrong he couldn't get back on course.

'At times Jacklin was badly advised. He continued to struggle in America, whereas, had he come back he could have achieved some success and built up to even more. A bellyful of failure makes it so much harder. He has had little peaks when he has played very well. The week of the 1977 Bing Crosby tournament at Pebble Beach he should have won—he was playing as well as anyone in the world. It was a tactical error not a lack of courage on the final hole when, after he had been driving so long and straight previously, he then took a one iron off the tee and the last hole became a dramatic anti-climax as he took six. I know he says he would do it again with a one iron, but I'm convinced that had he stayed with his driver he wouldn't have been stymied behind the tree on the fairway—he might not have got on the green in two, but he could have made a safe five which would have been good enough. He was thinking wrongly because he had been a long time away from that position.

'One of the keys to Jacklin's success was that he was very much inspired by the externals such as the roaring of the crowd egging him on. He was the man for the big occasions. Lately, he has not been getting any inspiration from anyone, and playing in the small stuff puts him at a disadvantage, especially at eight in the morning with no one watching. He's just grinding it out and in that mood he is very susceptible to camera clicks and crowd behaviour that would never have bothered him in the old days. Just imagine when he was winning at Lytham, the distractions there—you could have fired a cannon and he wouldn't have blinked.

'Jacklin had tremendous emotional appeal. We all wanted our boy to do well because that is what sport is all about. That's why people flock to football matches, to live vicariously through these athletes. It was the same with Jacklin. We all loved it and were terribly sad when he stopped giving us these kicks.

'At this moment there is certainly not another golfer in Britain who can compare with him as a striker of a golf ball. If he can regain his appetite for the game, he could come back. I don't think he'll get back his appetite—he'll settle for squeezing the last drops out of his past glories and cash in on all the commercial opportunity he can find. He's got enough to live on comfortably for the rest of his life and he wants to secure the future for his kids, which is very laudable—why not? I think he's willing to sacrifice his own career to that end now.'

John Ballantine, tennis writer for the *Sunday Times* and golf writer (Alex Lancaster) for the *Daily Telegraph* from America in the winter months: 'I think Tony was carrying the weight of the British national inferiority complex and this, with the fact of him becoming a great national hero, was almost too much for any one man to bear. It was far greater than in America where they probably have 20 golfers as great as Jacklin and they take it all much more objectively. They don't put a fellow on a pedestal the way we put Jacklin on one. Even the most realistic thinker like myself took great pride in the fact that he won those two great titles and showed the way to the Americans. I went along with the common Briton, thinking he was almost God. When he showed he had natural and normal feelings, and difficulty in keeping on top–I felt a bit cheated myself and the general public felt it more strongly than I did.

'With all the headlines–he was lauded to the sky when he won the first Jacksonville Open, then the two Opens–it was too much for any one man to take. The American writers just laugh at the way the British Press personify their great golfers as though they were winning wars instead of just winning competitions. The Americans never do that. They put Nicklaus in the correct spot. Over here the *Daily Express* has a headline, "Jacko does it for Britain" with two Union Jacks either side of the page– and the Americans just fall about laughing.

'To be fair, it's always been a bit traditional over here–we've always treated our sport in this manner. Playing a Test Match in war-time you would read, "England are losing and in dire trouble" and you'd think we were losing the war, but we're losing a cricket match.

'In Jacklin's case he was hailed as the one great post-war hero, beating the Yanks all off his own bat. Out of nowhere, there's this Lincolnshire lad who's winning the titles and we go overboard. Eventually he personified the whole menage making too much of him, then turning and rending him when he blew it, lost his nerve, or cracked under the strain of the whole Press expecting him to win. Everytime it's been the case. Whenever he has looked like doing something it's, "Is Jacko going to come back?", "Is Jacko a great champion?", until eventually everyone is up to the eyeballs in it.

'Of course, golf's the one game where the strongest man is proved to have the weakest nerve in the end–because he's used up all his nerves. Ben Hogan is the classic example of that. Sam Snead had to go to side-saddle putting. Arnold Palmer is sometimes pitiful on the greens. Why should Jacklin be any different?

'Probably he has a softer streak than Nicklaus, Trevino, Casper or Player–he hasn't got that touch of fanaticism. I've heard Tony talking about having a nice comfortable life, and his lifestyle has borne it out. He's indulged himself with that big fancy home in Gloucestershire, the large staff, the super Rolls-Royces–as though he had to live up to that kind of image. Perhaps it wasn't surprising he had a tremendous fall. It's like a Pop star who gets excessively famous and excessively rich, and then only someone who's a hard-boiled performer knows that that is the very time to keep practising and working on new notes—as Sinatra did when he had one or two bad patches in his career. When you're at the top you must work harder than at any other time—the true champion knows that. Maybe Jacklin was a bit immature and allowed success to go to his head.

'One isn't too sure what lies within Jacklin. His wife, Vivien, says he's as competitive as anybody, he wants to win as much as Gary Player or he tries as hard as Jack Nicklaus. But does he? Does he put in the time on the practice ground? No, he doesn't. I've seen him out there sometimes just larking about. He practises about 10 minutes and then starts acting the fool, knocking the ball over the fence, walking at the ball, chatting to anyone who will talk to him.

'We all admire him so much that we've really put him up there, as though he's got no vices. But I think he probably has ones we don't know about, and one of them might be that he hasn't got the right stuff in him to be a champion over a long period. He was a little bit of a flukey champion. Although he should have won two or three more big ones, he was only there for about five or six years. To have sustained it like Player or Trevino, coming back from terrific operations—that's the kind of fighter you need to be. I don't know whether Jacklin could have done that, whether he's got the stomach to do it.

'Tony's gift of the gab and his general Cagney-like manner gives you the impression he's incredibly tough, but I wonder whether he really is that tough. When he says, "if you think I enjoy holing those tricky down-hill 10-footers . . ." whereas a lot of the great players do enjoy it—Nicklaus enjoys doing that. Tony has been scared of it at times and would have liked to be back home sweeping up the leaves, or playing a round of golf and having a pint with the boys. That's his idea of a decent life.

'We don't know really what Tony's like—I suppose only Vivien knows that. I'm sure he cares about what has happened and I think he's a very emotional man. Certainly he's the most likeable man and I love the guy.

'People don't like to see their hero fall when he's supporting the whole of British pride and prestige on his back, then suddenly he seems to have feet of clay. People resent it. He was encouraged by the Press to moan, and when he was naive enough to alibi it out, people became disenchanted.

'When they criticise him in America, they just say he doesn't work hard enough. Tony rationalises that he did all the work as a young apprentice, got his game together working 10 or 12 hours a day and now he doesn't need to practise. That's all right if you're winning, but if you're in a terrible slump the American method is to work yourself out of it with sheer hard slog, not trust to luck and hope inspiration will come.

'Somewhere there's a lack of pride. He pretends to be proud, to want to do it again—but I wonder whether he does? He must be a bit spoiled by money, he's got it made. Then sometimes he rails against the public, the

Press and the criticism, without actually being prepared to kill himself to change it. He's not a strong enough character to really show the bastards–to work his way out of the pit.'

Tony on the Press

'Maybe I said too much to the Press but I don't regret anything that I've said to any of them. Over the years people have said to me, you say too much, you open up the book, you should close it a bit, let them wonder and think . . . but I'm not like that. The fact is, if I've been wrong all the time, why the hell do people still watch me? Obviously they don't believe all the stuff they've read.

'I may have talked too much, but I'm a product of what I feel and think, and I've always been willing to tell the truth as I've seen it at the time. Also, I don't think I have anything to hold back on what the Press have asked me.

'The thing that aggravates me is that I wonder whether they realise how important their job is, how they are influencing a terrific amount of people by what they write. The majority of the British Press are sensationalists to a large degree. They are hunting for stories–I know when they're doing it, when they've got nothing and no one to write about, and then they write things that in their opinion the public wants to hear. I question that.

'Frankly, I think the public are a lot smarter than the gentlemen of the Press give them credit for. They don't want huge headlines that mean nothing. They don't want sensationalism. It's rammed down our throats and has been overplayed throughout the media. Having talked to the public over the years, I know they are fed up with a lot of it.

'The Press take a quote, a sentence, a line–making a headline that is normally totally distorted from the true fact–just to attract you to it. You read it and think what a lot of bull.

'The Press use heroes as a tool to create interest in the media because they are not clever enough to give an analysis of a subject. It is far easier to take a topical thing or person and twist it.

'At one point I thought of writing to all the British newspapers saying why don't you have a golfer to write your column for you and give an unbiased opinion like Peter Thomson does in Australia. There are any one of a dozen British professionals who could do the job the Press do on reporting tournaments. And he'd have to do it right or he would have the wrath of all the other players descend on him.

'I could write as well as most of the Press fellows. It's only what they see through their eyes, and I'm never sure just how much they understand of what it's all about.

'I created an image through my golf, through my being on a golf course. If things were going well I was alive like an electric light bulb shining in the middle of the fairway and everything was going to happen. You get an atmosphere and there's magic there. I know I create it. I know people want to watch me, but not everyone wants to read about me all the time.

'To play the game, watch it, report on it–some of the things they write over the years about individuals–they are just terrible. They play golf themselves and they should know better. Like saying if you miss a short putt you shouldn't let it affect your game. Everyone knows that and it's easy to say but it's a very difficult game, and if it were easy, anyone could play. That's why you don't get many good players for a sustained length of time.

'I've been a target and at times it did get to me. I feel that the Press could have been a little kinder–not that they had any need to be–but the fact is that no other British player has ever done what I have done. They could have been more understanding. If they had said, he's trying to do too much, he's overworking, spreading himself too thin–that is the problem, which probably in retrospect it was. But instead they would say Jacklin blows it again, plays like an ass, lets down, or whatever knocking it was. It would have been better if they had taken an objective and truthful attitude, and said, when is he going to learn to slow down, he can't do as much as he thinks he can, instead of feeding the public what they assumed they wanted to hear.

'Because of what happened, I don't consider I have any real friends in the Press. That doesn't mean to say I'm not going to talk to them, because I realise it's part of my job. But over and above that, they mean nothing to me. They are something I have to put up with, part of an organisation which has to exist. I lost my respect for them in the last five years and I know if I win tournaments again in the next year or in the next five years, they will write all sorts of nice things. But that won't interest me either– it's too late. Some of them did a good job. Henry Longhurst was probably the most objective of them all, he really understood a lot better than most and he said on television that he thought the British Press had been less than kind to me.

'It's not just myself. I think the same goes for all our sports people– James Hunt, John Conteh or whoever. We have so few that have ever risen to world-class surely the Press should be the ones helping us to stay there, giving us confidence and a bit of advice. They could do that, they get around and meet people, they're not idiots.

'Inevitably when you're on the way up, you get good publicity, because they have a job to do. There are not likely to be bad articles about Nick Faldo or Severiano Ballesteros, as they are on the up and up, and it's marvellous. Being on the way up and getting there is one thing; maintaining a standard and staying there is a little more difficult. Rather than write knocking articles they should be writing constructively on what they have observed and learned from their experiences. I'm prepared to learn from anybody. As it happens I have had to learn the bloody hard way–the Press have helped me less than anyone.'

13: Through the Eyes of Other Players

IN GOLF IT IS relatively easy to measure yourself against the peers of your era, since there are major championships, tournaments and money that you win which put your achievements in a definitive order of merit each year.

The four majors are the most significant events in the golfing calendar. They are the Open Championship, US Open, the Masters and the PGA Championship of America. The importance of each major championship has, perhaps, a different meaning to each individual golfer. Certainly every British golfer primarily wants to win his own Open Championship. Most of Tony's energy in his golf career has been dedicated towards that one event. He was delighted to have won the US Open but maintains that he would prefer it to have been another Open Championship.

Jack Nicklaus, born 21st January, 1940, has made the majors his prime target and to date has collected a record 15 major titles–including five Masters–in the most successful manner of any professional golfer ever. He and other professional golfers have contributed to this book by giving their analysis of Tony Jacklin, the man and the golfer, relating it to their own experience in their golfing careers.

Jack Nicklaus

Jack Nicklaus is the one man whom Tony holds in the highest regard of any other professional golfer. Jack has dominated Tony's playing era and he has become a personal but not a close friend. Jack has shown sympathy and understanding to the younger man, and if Tony admitted to a hero in golf, it would be Jack Nicklaus.

Nicklaus was interviewed in the Press tent during the 1978 Open Championship at St Andrews, which he won. He apologised for not being more involved and forthcoming with his views on Tony, but explained that he could not give any more time during a major championship, which perhaps is indicative of the concentration that Nicklaus gives to his own golf when he is really out to dominate the event and achieve his goal. Without any doubt he is the greatest golfer of his era and arguably of any era.

'I like Tony very much, we've been good friends. Tony was a very good player back in 1969 and 1970, and then he made the decision to leave the American Tour. When he left the American Tour, I think he left his game. He left for financial reasons and I don't really blame him for that, because he could make more money playing outside America. He did better financially playing in Europe, but it didn't do his game any good. As a result I think it has been very difficult for him internally. He has had responsibilities being the first British golf hero for many, many years, and I really believe that he felt he owed it to the public to be in Britain. Yet for his golf he needed to be in America where the game was.

'Personally, I guess I have the desire, ability, determination, to continue to want to gear myself up to win, and I'm not going to make an excuse of something in my way. I'm going to get where I want to go, because I want to get there. If you want something bad enough you'll work at it and achieve it. Sure you might not make it, but at least you've given it your best effort.

'Maybe Tony has given it his best effort and he just can't make it. Maybe concentration is the problem that he has. When Tony first came to the United States, before he won anything, everybody felt he was going to be quite a good player and they were right. But then he left. I think he had the potential to be a continuing great player had he stayed. It's obviously very difficult when you don't live in America and that's where the golf is. Tony did what he thought he had to do by returning to Britain. I've never really had to play the majority of my golf out of my country— but probably I would have ended up playing some other game if golf had been outside America. Baseball has been big at the same time as golf. I was a good baseball player and had golf not been popular in so far as what I wanted to do in the States, then I might have ended up playing baseball.

'I continue to play golf because I enjoy it. I enjoy the competition, the game, being around golf and being part of it. I enjoy successfully competing. If I couldn't compete successfully or didn't enjoy it, I wouldn't play. I shall go on reducing my schedule to that end, so that the number of tournaments I play allows me to keep an interest and enables me to get keyed up for the major events.'

Arnold Palmer

Arnold Palmer, 50 years old in September 1979, was a golfing hero when Tony first came into the game. Palmer became one of the great golfing heroes of all time who provided the early inspiration for so many youngsters. Palmer's record includes three Masters titles, two Open Championships and one US Open win, but he lacks the PGA championship of his own country. His last major win was the 1964 Masters and he won a host of US Tour events from 1955 to 1973.

When Tony won his first tournament in America, the Jacksonville Open in 1968, he battled out the last two rounds with Palmer. Then Tony went on to become the closest we had in British golf to Arnold Palmer. He was the hero who set golf alight in Britain with fire, enthusiasm and that exceptional warmth of personality. He had the ability to communicate and reach out to the huge crowds who were attracted by the extraordinary magnetism of an individual, with whom they could identify, thrill to victory and suffer in defeat.

Arnold Palmer must be the best public relations man in the golf world. His natural talent for communication is outstanding and there are no feelings of animosity towards Palmer. He was interviewed at the 1978 Open Championship, first with a surrounding host of autograph seekers, then he moved away from the crowd and gave his full attention to talking about Tony.

'First of all, I think Tony was a great player. He still has the potential to continue playing as he once did. I'm not sure that he has the desire he once had to play. But he's at an age now where he should actually be at his very finest, he should be right at his prime. You never really know why or what happens to someone–I guess you could say the same about myself to some degree, although I have played a lot longer and I am a lot older. At a certain point you get tired and you lose some of your desire, some of the drive that you once had. At a Press conference recently, someone said to me, and I think the same principle could be applied to Tony: "What's different about you now than say in 1955?" Well that's almost a ridiculous question when you think about it. I don't care who the person is in a sport, whether it be Pelé in soccer or Borg in tennis, at some point when he has accomplished a lot, maybe not all the things he wants, so that he is still trying for them, his attitude changes greatly. First, nearly 25 years; second, in 1955 I was broke; third, I was in desperate need of accomplishing something so I had a great deal of desire and I felt like I had the talent if I could just put it to work for me. Like most young men at that age who are reasonably successful, I was very cocky–not really to the point that it was disgusting as I sometimes think now–but certainly I was. If there is a single thing you really need in addition to being talented and having a good golf game–you have to have confidence. An interpretation of that may be that sometimes you are thought over-cocky, but desire is very important.

'In Tony's case I can't be positive of what's going through his mind, but as I see him I don't see any real difference in his swing, or his putting stroke, or in him physically. What I can't see is what is happening to him mentally, and certainly that is probably the one thing that's affecting him. What is his desire? He may have lost his desire, but why?

'The pressure from the media and all the other commitments are part of what makes you tired, and in Tony's case he was the hero and probably still is to some degree, so he wants to get away and rest. He may not be able to do that because of the commitments he makes to himself and other people. Possibly someone who has handled that very well is Nicklaus, and of course Jack is strong in that he can stay away for three to four weeks at a time; whereas I think for Tony or myself or some of the other players, that is too difficult–we can't do that, we're just not built that way. We can't go away and leave it, but maybe Tony or I would have been better had we done a little more of what Jack does. On the other hand, we might not be able to play as well if we did that. There are so many unknown factors in this whole thing. But it's very obvious that mentally and physically you still want to do it, you still want to play. Your psychological mind says, well it's pretty well all over, and you're at that time or position where it's a matter of what can I do for myself now? I don't know the answer to that. I've got to believe that Tony wants to play well again. He's got all the things necessary to do so and it's hard for me to understand why he doesn't. I suppose only he can tell you that.

'It's not that difficult to travel from your own country to another to play. What's the difference in going to another country, so long as you're going? I've gone all my life. It's true that I don't stay for six months at a time, but then neither does Tony or Gary any more. But I know it's a problem and the more you stay home—particularly after a certain time of your life, that time being after you've been as successful as Tony has been —then it gets harder and harder to leave, especially for any great length of time. My family is all married and I'm still enjoying the playing, so I do just about as much as I want, as much as I can still enjoy.

'The pressure of everyone focusing on you is part of the whole business. There's no way of coping with it—relax and enjoy it is the only way to cope. Sure you get fed up. But that's when you get tired, so you go home and stay. The problem is that when you come back it is possible that you've lost some of that real driving inner force to win and to do well.'

Gary Player

Gary Player and Tony Jacklin are poles apart in temperament and personality, and each finds it hard to understand the other, and there is no reason that they should do so just because both are professional golfers. Player, born 1st November, 1935, from Johannesburg, South Africa, has golfing achievements that are highly impressive. He won the Masters in 1961, then in 1974, and he won it again in 1978. He needs another US Open title to complete a double grand slam of major titles. He has travelled the world playing golf, dedicated his life to it, believes that he should and is hard to assess as he always tends to go overboard about everything. When he was interviewed after playing a round of the 1978 Dunlop Masters, he was most anxious that he should be quoted exactly on what he had to say about Tony, so that his own image should be accurately interpreted. Certainly Gary is very sensitive to criticism—it's enough to fire him to win a tournament.

'You must try to reflect a man's personality when you write about him. When you get me, I try to be sincere and helpful. How many guys do you think are going to do what I do and put the effort into it? I do it because I've got to put something into life as well as take something out. My whole guidance in life is religion. What publicity do I need at my age? I've won everything. It doesn't tickle me to see my name in the paper, I don't get a thrill from that, I hardly worry about things like that.

'I want to make this absolutely clear, and I'm going to be 100 per cent honest. One man's opinion is not necessarily another's and I'm always reluctant to give an opinion on what somebody else should do. However, as you're asking me, I'll be honest and tell you. To me, Tony Jacklin's career is a great disappointment because I like the fellow very much. Tony has a fantastic personality, he's got a wonderful wife and family. I'm genuinely very fond of him.

'To me it's sad what he has done with his career, with his ability. Here is a man who won the Open Championship and the US Open when Britain was crying out for a champion. He came along, won the Open, and if you had to pick a person to win that title, you couldn't have picked a better person because he had the charisma, the looks, everything going for him. But I never saw a man go from so high to so low. Usually when they go that high they come down to three-quarters of the pace, stay there and come back again. He went as high up as he did, and that's how low he went – right to the bottom. And there's a reason for it. This is something I can give and not say it's my opinion, this is a definite fact. Tony and I used to have many discussions and I can remember sitting with him at the Lancome tournament in 1970 in Paris – he'd just won – and we were sitting waiting for the prize-giving to start, and he said to me, "why do you practise all the time? I sit here in the clubhouse every day, and I see you beating balls, beating balls, beating balls." I said, Tony, things are going very nicely for you now, but you'll remember the day when we were talking about this. You will realise one day when you don't play so well any more – and I didn't think it was going to come so quickly – how important practice and hard work are. He said, "Well, I don't agree with you, all this game is really, is tempo." If tempo were the answer to the game, everybody would be a champion. It's a lot more than just tempo. Basically Tony's got confused. He plays in Britain, then says he wants to go to America. He goes there and says he wants to come back home, and that's all because he lost the ability, this flair for his good play. I am convinced in my mind it came about through not practising hard, being lazy.

'We all have different opinions on what champions are – the different categories – a Jack Nicklaus, an Arnold Palmer, Ben Hogan or Sam Snead. Tony has never been that type of champion. It's a wonderful effort to win the two Opens, but that's in another bracket. You have three categories – classic and fantastic, good, and champion. He's in that champion group, not in the Nicklaus, Palmer, Hogan group. For Britain he was a champion. To me it's a tragedy, and I say this only in my eyes, that for this great country, Britain, he had done all this and he just let it go. I can't help feeling he owed it to the people, to this country – because after all they made him rich – to keep it going, keep that Union Jack flying. I'm fond of the man and I only want to say in this book what I'd say to him personally – and I have said it to him.

'Staying home because of his family is a lot of hogwash. If he'd kept playing as well as I did in America, he'd still be there today. He didn't need to live in America to be a top player. He didn't work enough on his swing so his game deteriorated and he had to get out of America because he was eating beans. I don't think there was too much pressure on him from the Press. There aren't any excuses at all – it just comes back to what I said – he was basically very lazy.

'I go on achieving because I still feel a young man. It's a crime in my opinion, a sin, when you've been given a talent in life and you don't use it – there's nothing worse, it's ridiculous. To me, that's a slap in the face to God. I'm grateful for the talent He's given me and I'm going to use it. When I'm old and I can't win any more you won't see me on the circuit, like a lot of these golfers who just plod along. But as long as I play well and have a chance of winning, I'm going to continue to play.

'I don't feel guilty about my family because they travel with me, it's a great education for my children. I go home for two months a year on my farm and I don't play golf, I'm with my family. I play golf with my son, watch my daughters partake in other sports, watch another son play rugby. I have a close affection with my family, and when you think that the average man goes to work at eight, comes home at six, well I spend just as many hours with my family. If you arrange your life correctly you can do these things.

'Nothing lasts forever. Let me give you a great saying: the talent that one has is only loaned to you, it's not permanent, it can be taken away this afternoon.

'I think I've given you plenty there to write.'

Lee Trevino

Lee Trevino, born 1st December, 1939, and a Mexican-American, exploded on to the golf scene. He joined the US Tour in 1967, won the US Open in 1968, and again in 1971. He won consecutive Open Championships in 1971 and 1972, and took the American PGA title in 1974 but the Masters still eludes him. With a terrific line in patter, this fast-talking, wise-cracking, very talented and strong golfer is a great favourite with the crowds. He rarely stops talking on the golf course, which is his way of releasing the tension, and the drama of his chipping into the hole and devastating Tony in the 1972 Open at Muirfield is almost to be expected from such an explosive character.

Trevino was interviewed at the 1978 Open Championship, after he had finished a round. He was surrounded by a fair gathering of people, with an even larger crowd waiting to pounce as he walked out, to ask for his autograph. He likes to play to the crowd, but he also attends very carefully to what you say and his rapid, shrewd response covers a lot of ground in a very short space of time.

'I don't know Tony that well. I've never had dinner with him, I've played very few practice rounds with him, really the only way I know Tony Jacklin is when I see him in the locker room and I say hi, Tony –

that's about it. Naturally I'd be a damned fool to say I wouldn't think good of him as a golfer. A lot of players come and go, it all depends on the determination of an individual, on what type of sacrificing an individual wants to do. We've all gone through it some place in life. A lot of times a person is guilty of being successful quickly and patting himself on the back instead of keeping up with the practising and concentration.

'He was the first British player in 18 years to win the Open. The people in Britain are great golf fanatics in the right way. They have more knowledge about golf because 90 per cent of the spectators at a tournament in Britain play golf, in the US only 40 per cent may play. It had to be very tough for Tony when he won the US Open after the British. The toughest thing to cope with in the game of golf is people – the Press, writers, newscasters, TV and radio. That is probably the thing that you have to really accept more than playing, or the competition. It's the other people who mean that someone like Tony hasn't any time to himself. He can't go out to eat in a restaurant without someone coming over, and you don't want to be rude and run everyone off, simply because you'd be cutting your own throat with all the commercials you do and things you endorse. I realise as much as anyone that it's going to happen to you if you're successful, but certainly that's the price you have to pay.

'After doing that for a long period of time he was affected by it and was not playing well. It's happened to me, to a lot of people, never to Jack Nicklaus because he doesn't play as much as Tony and I were playing. As a result Tony started avoiding people, avoiding the Press, and by doing that he stopped coming out in public, and when you do that you can't play, you can't practise. Instead of going out to the practice tee and spending three to four hours there, he wasn't doing that because he knew he was going to run into some sports writers, TV interviews, or autograph seekers, and he didn't feel like doing that. By avoiding it, he neglected what got him there in the first place which is hard work.

'Now it has lightened up on him and he'll make a come-back to the top again, simply because he's going to start going out again, practising again, and people are not going to be bothering him as much because he's not in demand at the moment. It happened to me. I had three bad years, a bad back, an appendectomy, and I got hit by lightning. But I wasn't called to the Press room after every round regardless of what I shot, whereas I had been there when I was doing well. When that happens, you have more time for yourself and you can start spending more time with what got you there in the first place. It's the toughest thing in the world to cope with, but it's the price you pay. You have to do these things as that's where you make your money – the money we make playing golf is only to pay the taxes on the money we make doing everything else.

'It won't be long before Tony Jacklin will be right back where he started again. Then he may do it a bit differently. Maybe he won't play as much. But when you're on top you have to do the constant interviews, the TV and radio. You're writing a book and if I weren't here talking to you, you'd have to leave out this chapter. But everyone has to make a living and it's very rude when you say, to hell with you, I'm not going to talk to anybody.'

Peter Thomson

Peter Thomson, born 23 August, 1929, and from Australia, has the enviable record of five Open Championship titles including a hat-trick from 1954, and then another victory in 1958 and again in 1965. Thomson went to America but rejected their Tour and way of life, concentrating his efforts on building an Australian tour, playing there and in the Far East, and making his very considerable mark in Britain.

Peter was interviewed, almost on the run, during the 1978 Colgate PGA Championship at Royal Birkdale, as he made his way towards the clubhouse. He was not loquacious but his opinion adds to the picture.

'I don't want to comment on Tony's performance. I decline to comment on his slide–that's his business. He emerged as the first young British boy with Australian cheek, and I'm sure he got this from his association with Bill Shankland at Potters Bar. If you talk to Tony he would tell you that Shankland was a very hard taskmaster, but also possessed that Australian pugnacity. Tony was never the cap-in-hand type, he had the cheek that you normally associate with Australians and I'm sure that was responsible for him achieving what he did. In terms of achievement, I don't know where he ranks as a golfer–he's a problem.

'In the case of young people in sport, they need an ego which is out of the ordinary. There hasn't been one golf champion who made it, who didn't have that. In Australia it's a sort of national challenge to distinguish yourself at some kind of sport, otherwise you don't rate and there's a lot of importance put on it. Ball games are the highest category– running, jumping and standing still are the lowest, that's why we don't do any good in athletics.

'At the time I was doing it, golf was just a normal day to day, week to week activity–you played golf and tried to win. At the time I also had the super ego that you need to stick your head up above the mob, and unless you have that you don't do it, no matter how talented you may be.'

Peter Oosterhuis

Peter Oosterhuis, born 3rd March, 1948, and from Dulwich, London, is probably the most likeable man in professional golf. As a golfer, he has achieved a great deal, but when it comes to the crunch he seems to lack that hard, ruthless streak, and the ability to dominate a field of world-class competitors. He has come close to winning the Open Championship and the Masters, but only close. He was a great rival to Tony when he joined the European Tour in 1970, and topped the Order of Merit for four years from 1971, believing all the while that week to week he was the best.

Gary 'The more I practise the luckier I get' Player shows why he's the world's greatest bunker player.

The man who talks about it, Peter Alliss, shares a joke with the man who still tries to do it.

When he went to live and play in America in 1974, he had to re-set his sights for the toughest Tour in the world, since when he has been doing reasonably well but falling below his own golfing standards.

Peter was interviewed in relaxed fashion and was actually the only professional who was sitting down as he talked at the 1978 Colgate PGA Championship at Royal Birkdale. He is highly articulate, always gives a considered opinion, he is willing to stick his neck out if he thinks he's right, and is very fair in his assessment.

'Unfortunately people are all too quick to forget what someone has achieved. I think it's probably natural, and it is worse in America than it is in Britain. If you win a tournament, two weeks later it's all forgotten – everyone is thinking about the present, and I suppose that is the way it should be. Tony won two major championships in the space of a year and not many people have done that. He was given a lot of stick by everyone over here when he didn't carry on playing at that standard, which I thought was a pity. Obviously he hasn't played well over the last three or four years, so that people are all too ready to say he's making a lot of money from different things and doesn't work hard enough at his golf. I'm not saying that I don't know why he doesn't play as well as he used to, nobody can answer that.

'We've forgotten what he meant to British golf at the time he won those Opens. He was "it" for four to five years, from 1967 through 1972 he re-vived British golf. When I was leading the Order of Merit, okay I was leading the points, but Tony had won the major championships. His game hasn't been the same since, but people were quick to write him off. I enjoyed our rivalry because in day-to-day tournaments I was coming out on top for a few years. When you treated the circuit as a whole I was achieving more than he was. But all the way along he'd won the two majors, did well in a lot of tournaments, and I was the one who was con-sistent week in, week out. I was prepared to grind it out and I could make a good finish after a couple of scrubby rounds – I'd make the most of it. Tony was more inspirational and if he could win was inspired.

'Ideally, to play in America full time, you should live there. When you're successful on the golf course then everything seems great, as it did in the early years for Tony in America. I think that quite a few of the players over there resented him doing so well. Their animosity came out because he was so successful. I haven't felt that at all, but they're prob-ably quite satisfied to see me hacking around – it's great! I've become one of the guys who makes the top 60 and does all right, but not well enough to hurt the home players' feelings.

'One reason for Tony's decline as a player could be that he always had a fantastic ambition and then all of a sudden he realised that his target wasn't there any longer, because Jack Nicklaus had achieved it or was holding it and Tony's ambition declined. Nicklaus had tremendous talent, he worked hard at it, and that's why he's the best.'

Henry Cotton

Henry Cotton, born 26th January, 1907, won the Open Championship three times, taking the title in 1934, 1937 and then again in 1948. He never won in America but he was the British professional who raised the status for professionals, though he had to go away to a job in Belgium and then come back to win his first Open Championship in order to do it. Henry has a place in golf where he can look back over the greats of a long period of time. He is lucid, opinionated, and it's good to have someone around who sees the whole spectrum.

Henry was interviewed between commentating on television at the 1978 Colgate PGA Championship at Royal Birkdale. He took time and trouble to give a reasoned opinion, 'I must get it right for a book' he said.

'Is he just a firework, a rocket that went up into the sky and then that was the end of it? Well, there's no question that for a brief period Jacklin was a sensational golfer. I've always seen him as an inspirational player rather than a working, steady type of professional. Billy Casper would be the professional's professional, who would always put on a solid show and if he didn't win he would still be right up in the top section giving good value for money. Jacklin would give a whole show with a bonus thrown in, or he would be a very mediocre performer. He never set out to get a series of fours and threes, he was always forcing birdies and pars, attacking as it were. I've never seen golf as a game that you can attack – it's so humiliating that if you really push it, even if you're the greatest player in the world, you can still have terrible disasters if your luck runs out. But Jacklin could play all the shots, he was very talented and I think his big successes were when he had putting spells which were uncanny. When he won the Open at Lytham I think he single-putted about seven times in the last nine holes, which is an unbelievable feat. On the other hand, you could say that if he needed seven one putts, he wasn't striking it well enough; but what can you say when a chap wins? I think Jacklin was a very good putter. Of course putting is only confidence and probably he got a big dejected when his game ran badly. When things aren't coming off he is the sort of fellow who might get a bit depressed. I don't say he would sulk or wouldn't go on fighting, but would lose a bit of heart.

'People give explanations about too much money and that he didn't practise enough. But I think everyone has to set a pattern of what he needs to do himself to hold his form and it's very difficult to know what that is. When you lose it, the thing you look for first is what you did when you played well. You can't say, I'm going to do a certain thing all my life, because that only works if you make allowance for your age. Every minute, every second, you're getting older, and I don't think you can follow anyone else on what they do, life must teach you. I've known people over the last 50 years, fellows who have a great triumph, win incredible matches, become champions and then 10 days later – it's gone forever, though perhaps no one realises until 10 years later.

'Jacklin was a fabulous player and I don't know how one would have advised him to do anything different. There was no reason to–he was great, he was winning, and making a fortune. He had people to advise him, who laid up his future for 10 years in terms of contracts and appearance money. He lives very comfortably and he's probably got an assured income. He has a nice family and all the obligations that go with it and I think he would do the same thing again, he wouldn't change that. The only thing we pick on him for is the fact that he doesn't win any more. I don't know whether one can say he's run out, like a doctor who qualifies and then never bothers to study any more, just stays put. Jacklin's got a living assured and a lot of assurance, he speaks well, he obviously understands the game. But I don't know what his future will be.

'The wear and tear between playing in Britain and America may be unnecessary, though Gary Player has proved it can be done by travelling non-stop for the past 20 years, but he's an exceptional fellow. Determination and concentration make a champion, and physical strength. A champion who stays good for a decade or even two decades, like Player and Nicklaus, means that you have a way of disciplining yourself. You can't live a ragged life, you have to establish a pattern and behave yourself. Although you get people who break all the rules, do everything to excess and seem to stick it. It all depends what you want out of life.

'Money is the incentive in golf now. In my day you came really for the honour–money was the objective, but you wanted to win the thing. It was like a degree. You got the paper stamped, passed the exam and your pride then drove you on. I was a bit ambitious and able to concentrate, and it's like that old thing about greatness: some are born great, some make themselves great, and some have it thrust on them. I suppose in golf you can make yourself great if you're lucky. On the other hand, sometimes you become a famous player because three other chaps collapse at the 18th, take three putts on the last green, and you've played well but haven't deserved to win. The doors open and you're let in. That can happen once in a fellow's life, but then he can never repeat it.'

Peter Alliss

Peter Alliss, born 28th February, 1931, had a marvellous record in a golf career stretching through the fifties and sixties, and finally got out of the game partly due to the fact that putting had become an agonising feature of it. One of the best strikers of the golf ball in the country, he had to live with the image of a great professional golfing father–Percy Alliss–and then his putting, which became a phobia. Now he is the best and most entertaining of television golf commentators. His interests are wide, his humour, and particularly his sense of the ridiculous, are delightful.

Peter was interviewed between commentating at the 1978 Colgate PGA Championship, and expanded at length in a warm and helpful manner on a subject to which he can relate closely.

'It was quite remarkable how Tony started off by winning those two championships–the style in which he won them and the confidence seemed to ooze from him. At the time many of the wise heads said, he'll disappear from the scene for 18 months while he capitalises on it. Then we all waited for him to come back again. He promised a couple of times, but it's gradually been a downward path which is hard to understand. The longer that downward trend has gone on, the more he has searched to try to find what he was doing before. I'm sure he's gone back through all his old clubs, old methods, old thoughts, and old clothes–when I had that pullover on I played well–and none of it is working.

'I feel he ought, if he can, to virtually start again and go back to square one as if he'd never won a tournament before. He should just try to put together a good round. He's trying to force everything, trying to do four under par and he doesn't need to do that. It's very sad for Tony most of all, and it's sad for the game that he's in such a state. You watch him and he's playing at the wrong rhythm–he walks too fast, hits the shots too quickly, it's all gone away. It's like being able to make omelettes all your life, then suddenly you can't–they come out like a lump of concrete.

'Certainly he was grossing a lot of money at one time and then he lost a lot through buying his house in the Cotswolds and maybe losing £70,000 out of earned income, which is a lifetime's savings for most people in the world. He's now living in Jersey and I don't know whether he's invested enough to live in the style, for the next 40 years, to which he's become accustomed and educate three children. But I don't think it's the soft living that has put him away. I think he's got befuddled with his own thoughts. Other people have played in and out of America, but basically Jacklin is a European and very English–he likes so many of the things in England, and he's got it into his head that it's impossible in America. You can travel and have a family and be away from home a hell of a lot. It does put a great strain on the family, but Tony's been very lucky in having a magnificent girl who has been a great help. If you want to see your youngsters grow up you've got to spend time with them, you can't give them a fiver to buy ice cream and then pat them on the head. It's a very complex picture and I'm sure 50 people would give you 50 different answers. I hope he finds it again, dammit he's only in his thirties.

'I don't understand why players disappear. You'd think once you learn how to play and you have confidence and fitness that you could go on. Whether he's able to admit it or not, obviously Jacklin's confidence has gone. It's the difference between someone who is not afraid of the dark, who is prepared to walk through any graveyard at one in the morning and not let it bother them; or another person who is frightened to go out into an open space and you say, don't be such a damned fool. But if you are, you are, and he's in that stage now. You can almost see an embarrassed look on his face as he goes to the practice ground. It's very difficult and very sad.

Left: *Tony with Henry Cotton at Penina, 1970.* Right: *Three men whose lives have all touched Tony's. Gary Player, Peter Oosterhuis and Tom Weiskopf playing in the 1978 Open Championship at St Andrews.*

'In an individual game like golf, there is a world order of merit and the number that can get to the top is limited. I know with Gary Player, so many people, including myself, said that he couldn't play, wouldn't do it, and he's gone and done it, which gives him an enormous kick. But it's got to come to an end some time and you can only be the best of your time. You go up the scale, remain at a peak and then must come down again. In a way it's an ego trip. At the end of the day, so much of life is conscience. If you have too much of a conscience, it's as bad as not having one at all.

'Tony has tried everything. Not practising, practising a lot; hitting balls in the net in the garden, making his own putting green, putting on the carpet. The longer it goes on the more difficult it becomes, because he's going to get himself in a winning position and the nerves come into it then and whether you can control them. When you haven't been in a winning position, and you suddenly need 4, 4, 4, to win, the fairways narrow, the greens seem to go further away and it's all down to you. The swing and tempo must remain the same, you should actually look as if you're enjoying it and then you're three or four up before you start. I don't know how Tony's going to get over it, but only he can do it.'

14: Thoughts on Contemporaries

TONY MAINTAINS THAT he has little interest in what his fellow professionals are like because he is too wrapped up in his own existence.

According to Tony he did not have heroes when he was young, yet he was definitely inspired in those days by players such as Ben Hogan and Arnold Palmer. Now, he positively enjoys the fact that he can tell you: 'I've played with every great player who is living.'

He has compared his situation to that of Gary Player, in as much as they were both outside the American sphere of golf. He has been influenced by Jack Nicklaus and wondered at the strength of his motivation. He is surprised by the constant good Press accorded to Arnold Palmer.

Tony admits to being curious, and in his own way he has made an extensive study of the professionals around him. He is observant and perceptive in his summary of them.

'I've never really wondered about my fellow professionals, on what motivates Jack Nicklaus, or what Gary Player does. I remember I once asked Arnold Palmer about the backswing. I know what the other guys are doing, from watching them. I promise you that if I wanted to know something from them I'd ask – but it doesn't interest me.

'I am more interested in what I do. I know that within me I have the ingredients for greatness. I've put 35 years into myself and I'm having a hell of a lot of fun sorting me out. I'm really occupied and it's great.'

On Arnold Palmer: 'I know how he feels with the galleries, with people, and I can relate to certain similar situations. He had that marvellous ability to do what he did – hitch his trousers, walk the fairway, waggle, and he did it all without it affecting his game. You can't meddle with the ingredients of success. He sensed what people wanted and he gave it to them and they loved him for it.

'Arnold is so full of himself that he doesn't help anybody. He wouldn't tell anyone anything to make them feel any better, because he wants to go all the way to make himself feel as good as he can.

'I say it in the nicest possible way but he's got the biggest ego of anyone I've ever met.

'He still makes so much money, it's extraordinary. They say he makes £10 million a year, which is incredible.'

On Jack Nicklaus: 'Nicklaus is the greatest player that ever lived and I have great respect for him. The reason I like Nicklaus more than anyone else when it comes to the great players, is that he's the only one who is a human being with it. I hold him in the highest esteem.

'I know that I said I wanted to be the greatest player in the world – and I was close to it at one time – but I didn't know exactly what I meant, whether it was for hours, for minutes, or what – it's just something one says. To be considered is important, and I realised that Nicklaus was always going to have that "greatest" tag.

'He was clever to concentrate on winning the majors. That was a very smart decision. I'm not knocking them in any way, but the majors are the easiest ones to win, in the sense that you eliminate a higher percentage of the field from being in contention.

'It's incredible to be able to make that decision and then go out and do it, especially as he didn't need to financially.

'I was at Jack's house when he won the 1971 US PGA Championship at West Palm Beach in Florida. I went fishing with him every day, and one day we came in and a woman who was there, said to him, "Well done Jack, you really needed the money." She was half-serious, half-joking. Jack said, "God dammit, don't you realise it's not the money, it's being the best player." Of course she didn't understand, and it was sad.

'That's the way it is with him – it's the game, and he never loses sight of that fact. Above all, it's a game to be played and enjoyed in a good spirit. If you can do that, play in that light, you're going to be a better person for it.

'It's sick to me that people want to see a guy like him topple – it's bloody masochism. I don't understand it. Maybe I'm an idiot, but I feel that those people don't know anything about winning, losing, and the game – they are just stupid. They're not worth anything, and they will never rise to a higher level of understanding. It gets up my nose and I don't need them. They are sick people, not well-balanced, it's that simple. I'd rather talk about something else, because it just aggravates me.

'Golf is about good thinking, being good in your life. That is important. You're not afraid and you don't have guilt about things. To thine own self be true – many clichés would be suitable. But you can't deviate from that, and I've met very few at the top who are not good in that sense.

'Certainly Nicklaus is above any petty thoughts, and that's why I regard him as highly as I do.'

On Ben Hogan: 'I played with Ben Hogan in a practice round in the last tournament he entered, but he didn't play, due to a bad leg.

'Jackie Burke came and asked me if I'd like to play with Hogan the following day, and I said, yes, of course. The next morning I was on the putting green and Terry Dill, another professional golfer, came up and said, "Have you all got a game? Have you all got four?" I replied that I didn't know, I would check.

'I went over to Ben and said, do we have four? He said, "Who's asking?" I told him it was Terry Dill. "We're fixed," said Ben. So then we proceed to tee off in front of Terry as a threesome, and I felt like a real ass.

'We played four or five holes and I'd forgotten all about it. Ben came over to me, and suddenly out of a clear blue sky he said, "He came up to me once before.' Who? I asked. "That Terry Dill; he came up to me on a putting green, and he said, Mr Hogan, how do you get your mind in shape to concentrate and prepare for a major championship? Do you know what I replied? I told him the first thing was that I didn't come up to talk to other people on the putting green."

'Hogan smiled and enjoyed that as he told me; he thought it was smart, terrific.

'The more one gets to know these so-called geniuses, the more pleased I am to be me. To be honest, I know I'm opinionated, but I wouldn't say anything as bloody silly as Hogan did to Terry Dill. I don't get any joy in putting people down.

'I didn't show Hogan any more respect than I felt was due. A lot of guys go and lick his boots. I don't believe in that, I never did.

'I think he's just another person and not a particularly nice one at that. He certainly doesn't go out of his way to improve his image with other people. Individuals like that haven't got much consideration for their fellow-men.

'Hogan was a superb golfer and, when I played with him, I could see that technically his capabilities were still all there.'

On Sam Snead: 'Sam is the greatest character of them all. He's human– like Dai Rees, who is a marvellous, fantastic chap. To have gone through what Sam has in his life as a professional–I know what it means–and he must have had some terrible times with his putting. But in his outlook he's still like an 18-year-old. He still wants, more than anything else, to play golf, be young, be one of the boys. We both love jokes and telling gags.

'I remember practising with Sam, and once we both stood on the practice tee and he said, fade, and we'd hit a fade or he said draw, and we'd both do that. Whatever shots he said, we'd hit them together.

'Then some time later he came and told me people had told him I didn't practise. He said to me, "It doesn't really take much practice," he was being nice. I thanked him for telling me, although I know that I've never gone out unprepared to play in any tournament.

'I like Sam. I would pick out him and Dai Rees in their attitude to life, although I don't know that I'd want to play golf that long.'

On Tommy Bolt: 'I played a lot with Tommy. I find that with people who lose their temper, who let the game get the better of them and go bananas–then I go overboard because it becomes so funny.

'I played in a tournament with Tommy and a couple of other guys when Tommy missed a putt and then started hitting the ball right round the perimeter of the green, as though it was an ice-hockey puck. He said, "You can't play this game if your ass is red, and I'm carrying my red ass right off the course." Then he walked in. It was hilarious.

'You could see the game getting the better of Tommy, taking over. He was mentor to Tom Weiskopf, who learned everything from him. It all

132

rubbed off on Tom and maybe it was what attracted him in the first place.

'Tommy Bolt was magic – but he was a perfectionist to the point where he was impossible.'

On Gary Player: 'Without any question, Gary Player is one of the most remarkable people you'll ever meet at any time in your life. His achievements in golf are nothing less than incredible and he's dedicated his whole life to being as good as he can possibly be. He has a genius, and I mean that in the fullest sense of the word, for getting the ball into the hole. He's certainly the best I've ever seen at playing the little touch shots around the green and, of course, he's accepted as the master of the bunker shot. In addition to that, Gary is one of the game's best putters from 10 feet and downwards and I doubt if any other professional golfer has holed as many crucial putts in that range as he has.

'I find his dedication to practice and hitting golf balls very interesting because for a very great player, he hits more bad long shots than any other player I've ever seen. He's been plagued with a hook all his life but it's strange that the part of his game he practises the most is, by far and away, the worst. I would think he learned the short game as a youngster and it's stayed with him all his life.

'Perhaps all the hard work he puts in on his long game does something for him in the way of motivation or maybe he sees it as a price he has to pay for the success he's achieved – I don't know.

'I know he thinks I'm lazy. He went out and believed in his fanatical way that you had to beat balls all the time. I haven't the same mind. I have broad horizons, whereas he has tunnel vision. I have a whole world out there.

'We're totally different. I know he hasn't any respect for the way I do things. He thinks I've made a complete cock-up of my life. I don't happen to think that's so. I've got out of my life what I wanted. I'm not saying I've been happy over the few past years playing golf the way I have. But it wasn't easy to try to explain to people that I had a mental block in putting and what caused it was a situation that arose because the public wanted me to win so much, and I was trying too hard.

'Gary is going to grind himself into the ground, he's such a fanatic. His talent has been unquestionable. I'm not jealous of the guy at all, because he has nothing I want, but I'm totally opposite to him in my thinking – not about the desire to win – but in having other areas which interest me.

'Gary is so darned dedicated to his own well-being. If someone says, Nicklaus is a great player, then Gary says, "Put it in your notebooks that I'm going to be better."

'Gary is 10 different people but he would always say well played to someone else; he would never *not* say it. He would say well done, and would notice if anyone didn't.

'Once in Australia, I saw him go up to Guy Wolstenholme on the putting green – Gary had just won the week before – and Guy and he were chatting.

Left: *The Bear-hug. Caddie Jimmy Dickinson is the recipient following his master's victory in the 1978 Open Championship at St Andrews.*

Right: *Tennis balls at 20 paces. Britain's leading golfers of the 1970s try another sport.*

Left: *Tony on Arnold Palmer: 'You can't meddle with the ingredients of success'.*

Guy never said, well done last week, and Gary, quite rightly said to him, "What is it with you? Does it really hurt you so much to say well played to another person?" Guy said, "No, what are you talking about?" And he was very embarrassed.

'But in that situation, I would have to think not to say well done. Gary had won the week before and we'd all been there.

'Gary doesn't give anything away, but he always congratulates another guy who has won.'

On Peter Oosterhuis: 'I've never met anyone I like more than Peter – he has great qualities.

'At the end of 1968, I became number one, but he was a far better player in Europe than I was. He was as good as you'll see on British golf courses – good at hitting the ball, finding it, getting it up and in. He really had the mind for it and enjoyed it.

'When it came to the yardage situation in America, he started to lose his feel and that was his greatest attribute. In the US, a lot of feel goes out of the game and you become very stereotyped.

'I was never happy with the comparisons made between myself and Oosty. The Press used it to make their job easier. There was an element of competition all the time; but I want to beat everybody, not Peter more than anyone else – in fact probably less than anyone else because of his understanding of the mind, and I like the guy – he's one of the nicest individuals you could ever come across.

'He hasn't a distorted view of golf. He's managed to maintain the pride in the job for himself. That's the objective, the true satisfaction, and he's never lost sight of it and I hope he never does.

'He's too nice a fellow to be going through what he is in America. I think he made a mistake in going. To be at the top over there, he hasn't just got to beat all the Americans, he's got to do it at a disadvantage, because it is not his background, his own environment.

'He's trying to beat the best who have been reared there, while for him it's a foreign land. I don't care what anyone says, it's not the same as being at home.

'He had to fulfil himself totally and felt he could never do that if he didn't give himself the opportunity to go and win where the best were – so he opted to live in America. If he's unhappy, he should admit he was wrong and come back. It's not admitting defeat.

'He's had a go over there, had the opportunities to win, and missed them. He must know he's not good enough to win five or six times a year, which is what you've got to do to make an impact.

'He's a potential wizard. His mind worked so well. When he hit the odd loose shot he knew he had to cope with it, and he did. It didn't matter if he was struggling to get down from off the green, he enjoyed that, it was fun.

'For him to beat the best in America is so very difficult. Even if he could play Nicklaus's game, he would still be out of his own environment.'

On Severiano Ballesteros: 'Ballesteros is a shot in the arm. He is just something else. He plays the game in the right spirit–smashes it long, ambles after it, looks for the hole, whack, and it all looks such fun.

'He gives you the feeling that he's actually enjoying it–and he is. You've got to have ability and the desire to want to be better than the rest.

'He's won in America, which was great, and it will be interesting to see what he will do there in the future.

'At the moment, he's doing it all and enjoying it, but when it gets too much, for whatever reasons, that's when the problems start. He'll not be human if he doesn't go through some form of what I've been through.'

On Peter Alliss: 'Peter is a professional who isn't any longer committed to playing. He sits and watches and when he comments on television, where the most important thing is that he is interesting to the public at large, he sometimes tends to forget just how difficult the game really is. He's very good at his job–the best–but it's easy to sit back and judge.

'I'm reluctant to judge; I always think, there but for the grace of God . . . you never know when something is going to happen to you. On television they pontificate, make light of things, but I'm out there in the pressure-cooker every day. I'm still very close to it.'

On Henry Cotton: 'He was a very good national player–he never won much anywhere else. The Open Championship was nothing like it is now– how many Americans came over when he won? I bet he never played more than seven tournaments a year. I've played 30 some years. I've played more tournaments at 35, than Henry did in his whole lifetime. People don't get things in perspective.

'Henry came up to me at a tournament one day, and said, "Hello Tony or is it the late Tony Jacklin? How did you manage to take six on that last short hole?"

'Henry, I said, I did it for fun. The day had been drab up to then and I thought, well I'd better make it a bit more interesting, so I took fucking six on the 18th. "So you're a comedian as well are you?" says Henry. Yes, I replied, I am when people ask me questions like that.

'I sometimes wonder whether Henry knows what he's saying. He's never bothered to put himself in someone else's position, to try to see it their way. Everyone is supposed to give up their whole life to the game of golf. Hogan was the same. I don't see the point in it. I want to enjoy other things and still play good golf. If I do it, and make a success of it, then I'm my own man and I'll have done it my way.'

15: Caddie Talk

SINCE 1967, TONY's regular caddies have been two level-headed Scotsmen and firm friends – Willie Hilton and Scotty Gilmour.

The fact that the caddie-golfer relationships survived a long time speaks well for all concerned. There are plenty of such relationships on Tour, not always easy to sustain, and some do come to an untimely end.

The Tour caddies are all individualists who enjoy the nomadic existence. Their lot has improved in the last 10 years, in that now there is slightly better provision for them at tournaments, which is largely due to their having become a much more articulate group.

The role of the caddie has changed somewhat, mainly through the total acceptance among professional golfers of pacing the yardage at every hole. Now, one caddie is designated to go round the course very early each morning before play begins in order to make a chart for all the caddies of pin placements on the greens, so that the distance to the flag can be accurately gauged to the last yard. However, some caddies do not find the charts satisfactory and still walk the course themselves.

Sometimes the caddie will pace the course yardage or the professional, when he plays a practice round, paces each hole using trees or hillocks as yardage markers. It is useful knowledge, but often it is more of a crutch to the professional than anything else.

Tony has never had a caddie to advise him on putting, on choosing the line to the hole. Many caddies would prefer not to advise on putting, though they will if asked. The caddie is really used by the professional as a prop and a sounding board. The player wants to reinforce his thoughts on yardage, what club he should use, or the line to the hole. The more advice a caddie gives, the more he lays himself open to blame, but that is an accepted part of the job and professionals vary in how much blame they apportion to a caddie.

Tony has probably become more of a moaner on the golf course over the years, but moaning from a sportsman is often frustration with himself at not being able to perform as he would like. Certainly Tony does not feel that his caddie is in any way responsible for his play.

Willie Hilton, from Glasgow and the father of five children, is an outwardly resilient fellow, and in 1967 he teamed up with Tony at a golf course where much was to happen in the life of the young British golfer – Royal Lytham and St Annes. 'It was the Pringle tournament at Lytham,' says Willie. 'And Jacklin won it. It was his first major win in Britain, and the first big one I'd won. The first prize was £750. From that tournament we developed a good friendship and an understanding.

'My lifestyle improved through working for Jacklin. I could buy thing[that I would never have had so quickly. I have done rather well out [golf, and being with Tony, people were prepared to employ me when h was in America, because they could be certain that I knew my job.

'I worked hard and I was paid for it. I did all the yardages, and we decided the club choice between us, although obviously the final decision was his. He might blame you if it's the wrong club, but it's the same with most professional golfers, although some guys will admit they have hit it wrong. Jacklin and I never had much trouble with clubbing, we had an understanding and he was pretty fair that way. I never read the greens for him, though I have for some other professionals.

'Jacklin was one of the best golfers I've ever seen – he could play all the shots, the three-quarter, quarter, full shots, and he was very, very good at the half-shot. I would reckon he's the best we've ever produced in big-time golf. He went and played the Americans in their own back yard and won, which is some achievement on its own. It was great to win those two Opens back to back, and the two Jacksonville Opens.

'The most exciting moment of my career was winning the Open Championship at Lytham – that was fantastic – the crowd was delirious and it was very electrifying. The most worrying moment of the Championship was after Charles had played a good shot out of the rough at the 18th, and put it about 20 feet from the pin. Jacklin's yardage for the last shot was an eight iron, but I thought he should go down the grip and hit a little seven, which he did under pressure when most guys would be backing up and hitting nine, because they were pumped up. Jacklin put his shot inside Charles, which shows the calibre of the guy. When I saw that, I thought – that's it. When it was all over I just felt relieved. I said to the late Henry Longhurst, when he asked me how I felt, that it was like bringing in the Derby winner and it was a great feeling.

'Another great experience was winning at Jacksonville in 1972, when I spent 14 weeks in America with Jacklin and really enjoyed it. He paid me a weekly wage and a percentage. Once we won – that was everything sorted out, although we had done very well earlier on the tour. We tied 6th in the Bing Crosby, tied 4th in the Phoenix Open where we were leading at one stage; tied 4th at Inverarry where we were leading with six holes to go, and then after winning Jacksonville we tied 7th at the Greater Greensboro Open two weeks later.'

The following year after the Open Championship at Troon in July, the split came between Jacklin and Willie Hilton. Tony, not wanting to cause offence or have a confrontation, told Willie he was going to train the son of a couple already in his employment in Gloucestershire to caddie, and to drive his car for him.

The manner in which Tony parted from Willie obviously hurt Willie deeply and did cause offence: 'Jacklin came to the back of the car after the final round at Troon. "By the way," he tells me, "that's it. I've got this guy that works in the house, and he's going to caddie for me." That was all he said. And to this day I don't know the reason. I think there was something else behind it, and I've heard mention of a few things, but he couldn't come to me and tell me.

'At the time, I said to him, what's the reason? What have I done that has made you come to this decision? He said, "you haven't done anything – why don't we just part the best of friends, we've been friends for six years." I said, well if that's the way you want it – that's it.

'There was no way I was going to sit down and cry, because without boasting I could go and work for anyone. But it was the suddenness of it. If he'd told me before that this was going to happen, or built up to it . . . that would have been different. To be told just there and then – it was a bit of a shock at the time. What I would like to know is, if we had won the Open, would we have parted?

'Well, you soon get over it because you can't rely on one guy for earning your living, there are plenty more fish in the sea. I reckon I'm as good as the next guy so far as caddying is concerned. Obviously, I felt it wasn't the right way to do it, but if that's the way the guy wants it – you're only the employee and he's the employer. It's the same in all walks of life, once they tell you you're fired, that's it.

'You can go and cry or think you've been done an injustice, but I didn't. I said, that's that. I got in the car, said a few unkind words and I can honestly say that in a week I was over it and back on the course. He was more worried than I was, because he thought I would foul-mouth him, but I never did that, never.

'I never socialised with Jacklin. When I finished on the golf course I wanted to go my way and he went his. Once the golf was finished I was away – I didn't want to hang on to him or walk about with him. The less you see of one another after the golf, the better.

'He never moaned on the course when I was with him, but it's different when you're playing well. I don't think he ever concentrated well and he was easily disturbed – unless he was pumped up and the adrenalin was really flowing, then he was good. He showed his best when he had a ding-dong battle, then he could play perfect golf. After three rounds he would say how many are we behind? I'd say four and he'd reply – okay we can win. He knew he could win and he went out and won.

'At the Wills at Dalmahoy in 1970, where he won by seven shots, he said to me on the 17th tee, what do I need to break 70 again? I replied, two threes – and he did it – shot 69 and broke 70 four times: 67, 65, 66, 69 – that was pretty good golf.

'I don't think he has changed, although maybe he was hungrier. Everyone reckons now that his putting has gone, but he was always the type of putter who blew hot and cold, he was never mediocre. Maybe with a long spell of not having won, he's trying too hard because he's desperate to win and that's affecting his game. Certainly it used to be that when he was hot on the greens no one could live with him.'

Scotty Gilmour, born in Girvan, Ayrshire, has a 14-year-old son. He is an easy going and emotional man who has been caddying for Tony mainly through his leaner period, and he has been a prop to him on the golf course, as well as becoming involved in a social and family sense. 'Scotty is clued up,' says Tony. 'He gets good yardages and he doesn't make mistakes, or if he does he admits them. He helps me occasionally with clubs, but doesn't read the greens because he reckons he does it in Chinese.

'I can take Scotty anywhere, introduce him to anybody, he knows how to act. He's a great guy and we've hardly had a cross word in six years. I hope it lasts a long, long time; it may not be forever, but I happen to like the guy very much. I know enough now to know that nothing is forever. I might change or he might. I feel comfortable with him, I know he's pulling for me all the time, he's always amiable and pleasant. Sometimes he drives for me. He likes the kids and has often been a babysitter.'

A master carpenter by trade, Scotty emigrated to Canada in 1964 and then went down to Florida in 1965 for the warmer weather and began as a Tour caddie, having learned caddying as a boy at Turnberry. He first met Tony in America in 1968, and used to follow him and got to know him. In 1972 he worked for Tony in America, and joined him in 1974 in Britain.

'Tony doesn't attack the golf course like he used to, he has become more negative, especially on the greens, which is killing him. He's hitting the ball so well it's unbelievable, but he puts so much pressure on himself on the greens. He looks scared when he gets over a putt and he takes the feel away from it. Concentration is part of it. If only he could stop the bad experience, shake it off for a couple of months, he could get it out of his subconscious mind.

'It's a real mind-bender and I think I'm going to crack before he does. He's got to do it, but there's as much pressure on me watching it and feeling it for every hole, every day, that it's a wonder I haven't got ulcers.

'He was never a great putter, always streaky, but with the bit between his teeth he could do anything. Now the whole world's against him. It used to be that if we picked a wrong club it wasn't a disaster. Now we can't do anything right and I resent the fact that he doesn't take responsibility. Sometimes the blame is put on the caddie even if the shot is hit badly.

'He's always been a tough job. I've caddied for Gary Player, Chi Chi Rodriguez, Dan Sikes, and even Bruce Crampton was an easier job than Tony. He expects you to be perfect and that puts an awful lot of responsibility on the caddie. He's very selfish on the golf course.

'We get on well on and off the golf course, but it's very nerve-racking when you know he's going to jump on you for the least mistake. He puts so much pressure on me and he doesn't realise it. I don't think any other caddie would have stuck it.

'America affected Tony's mind. It got to the stage where everything bugged him: cameras, people jingling change, he was looking for it all. Seven years ago nothing bothered him. Now it has all changed in his own head. It's not something that happens, you bring it on yourself.

'As a caddie you have to be with a winner to survive. It's a big gamble. I guess I'm just a fool. The professional can afford it – he's got contracts and endorsements. If Tony never wins again, it won't matter for him financially. I would just go down and down. I think Tony puts too much value on money – everything is money and more money. He still thinks £500 is a lot of money – I think it's nothing and I'm poor and he's wealthy. If I had the money he has, £1,000 would be like a fiver to me. I say to him, I wish I had your money and he says, you'd be broke in a year. I probably would be but its for spending – the last suit you wear has no pockets.

'Off the golf course Tony hasn't changed much, he's still a regular every-day guy. He likes the simple things in life. He enjoys and cares about his wife and children and he enjoys a good laugh, sometimes a drink and he forgets about golf.'

Sonny MacMillan, a Glaswegian and for many years Peter Townsend's Tour caddie, says: 'It's probably easier to work for someone on a short-term basis, as I did for Tony in 1975. I spent nine weeks with him on the American Tour, and he treated me like a king. He paid my air fare to Hawaii; he put me up at the best hotel, took me out to dinner every night; he gave me a lot of clothes. When we were in Phoenix we flew in a twin-engined Piper Comanche through the Grand Canyon – it was fantastic.

'He's not selfish. He does get a bit moody at times but he's one of the best guys on the Tour. On the golf course he gets uptight and he's a stickler for yardages and blames you if you're wrong. I never did anything for him on the greens – tournament golfers don't need anyone to read greens. You can give a guy a line, but you don't know how hard he's going to hit it. Tony's a hard man to work for in respect of his jumping on you, which he does because he's a perfectionist. When we were in America he was so keen to win it was unreal but he was trying too hard and was very uptight. He moaned when he had off-days and let it get to him.

'He's probably the best golfer Britain's ever produced. He's got the ability – his record proves it. You can fluke one major but not two, as well as two Jacksonville Opens. Nick Faldo is never going to do that. I don't think Tony's record will ever be equalled by a British golfer.'

16: The Ryder Cup

For Tony, the Ryder Cup is more a source of embarrassment than an event to be savoured. Because he is a highly individual personality, because at all times he prefers to be dominant, to be associated with winning and success in spite of his own game having taken a tumble, he finds it excessively hard to accept that he is going to be part of a side that is more likely than not to be the losers at the end of the day. Even if he wins as an individual – and his Ryder Cup record is reasonably good – he still hates the association with failure that being part of a British team can bring.

Tony has played in every Ryder Cup side since 1967 and the only one where he felt any real sense of enjoyment was in 1969, the year of his Open Championship win and the year the Ryder Cup was played at Royal Birkdale. It was an amazing scenario, and one where the final setting was dominated by the figures of Tony Jacklin and Jack Nicklaus.

'I've never really enjoyed the Ryder Cup because golf is too individual a sport. Inevitably if you play any good at all, you get in the team. The only time I've ever been inspired was at Birkdale in 1969 where it wasn't like a Ryder Cup at all.

'On the last day I played Nicklaus in the morning and in the afternoon. It was as though he and I were just playing match-play all day long. In the morning he wasn't playing very well and I beat him 4 and 3. After the morning singles had been played Great Britain had a two-point lead over the Americans.

'We were the last match out in the afternoon, and Nicklaus started to play better. By the time we reached the 17th, I was one down. I managed to win that hole by slotting in a huge putt right across the green, for which a cheer went up that was heard by Brian Huggett ahead on the 18th green, playing Billy Casper. Huggett thought I had won my match and that he needed to hole his putt from four feet, for the team to win. He holed it.

'As Nicklaus and I stood on the last tee at six o'clock that last day the Ryder Cup was all square and our match was all square. The match depended on the result of our game.

'I remember seeing Eric Brown, our captain, walking down the fairway with his hands in his pockets trying to look relaxed. Both Jack and I hit three woods off the tee, and then I rushed away, ahead of Jack and was walking along feeling really tight. Suddenly I heard Eric call, "Tony"; he caught me up, put his hand on my shoulder and said, "Are you nervous?" Am I nervous I replied, I'm petrified. "Oh," he said, "I thought I'd ask you. If it's any consolation I feel just the same way as you do." I laughed and said, isn't it a bugger? Then we walked down together.

'I hit my shot with an eight iron to about 30 feet, and he hit his to about 15 feet. I then left my 30-foot putt two feet short. He hit his five feet past, marked it, put it back and knocked it dead straight into the centre of the hole. He picked his ball out of the hole, picked up my marker, conceded my putt, and said, "I don't think you would have missed that putt—but in these circumstances I would never give you the opportunity."

'After that was the only time I ever put pen to paper and wrote to another professional. I said, your gesture on the 18th green was something that I'll never forget as long as I live.

'More than half of his team were bitching and going on about the fact that he gave me that putt. Nicklaus plays the game in a spirit above the rest.'

On other occasions the outcome of the Ryder Cup has not been so happy for Tony or the team. Over the years Tony has played under the captaincy of Eric Brown, Dai Rees, Bernard Hunt and Brian Huggett. His partnerships have mainly been confined to four other professionals. 'I think the pairings in the team are of paramount importance. Most captains have discussed them with the players, so that two fellows paired together shouldn't have any reservations about each other. It's certainly important to me. I enjoyed playing with Dave Thomas, with Peter Oosterhuis and I think Peter Townsend and I complemented each other. It was fun playing with Brian Huggett, he's a great trier and you know he's always giving 100 per cent.

'Eric Brown and I never had a lot to say to each other but I think he did a great job as captain. I don't mean in any derogatory sense that I didn't like him—it was just that Eric was an individual and so was I. I remember at the 1971 Ryder Cup at St Louis, Missouri, there was this American guy who picked me up at the airport in a Rolls-Royce just like my own. I was doing interviews at the airport, all the other players had gone in coaches which were chock-a-block full. I was a bit worried about this American meeting me, who had read that I had a Rolls-Royce at home and he thought it would be nice to meet me in one just like it. I told John Bywaters (then Secretary of the PGA) who was with us, and asked if it would be all right to go with this guy, as the coaches were full. He said it would be all right, so I went. Then Eric, who was captain, had a word with me at the hotel, telling me he didn't want me riding around in a Rolls-Royce while the team was riding in coaches. And he was in order. Although instinctively I felt—why should a team all go in a coach? Why is it that for one week out of two years you're supposed to suddenly act like schoolchildren? I understood what Eric meant and I tried to explain that I had asked about doing it, but I didn't argue with him at all.

'I always got on very well with Eric. As much as he was a hard man, I never felt unable to approach him or discuss things with him. You wouldn't be afraid to say–do you think that's all right–which is super. I don't think anyone should put themselves on a pedestal–nobody's that good. You have to remember you're dealing with individuals, that you must keep the players happy within themselves.'

When it came to the Ryder Cup played at Royal Lytham in 1977, the outcome was not at all happy, either in the defeat by the Americans of $12\frac{1}{2}$ matches to $7\frac{1}{2}$, nor in the personal sense for Tony. Brian Huggett was the non-playing captain of the team: 'He made up his mind for better or for worse that he wanted to be captain. He put himself forward for the post–no one else thought of Huggett until Huggett thought of himself.

'I thought he was still too good a player not to play in the team and when it came to the PGA Committee meeting of which I was a member, I voted against him and voted for John Jacobs. We agreed that if Huggett made the team he couldn't be captain–but in the event he was.

'I was very disappointed with the way Huggett handled the job and I doubted the wisdom of the way he did things. He didn't consult any of the players about pairings, he just did it in his room, in his mind, and I question whether that was very wise. I have nothing at all against him. I enjoy playing golf with him and I admire the effort he makes.

'I'm not implying that I would do a better job, or would be a great captain, but I wouldn't do it the same way. I would purely and simply try to be logical and talk to every player about whom they feel comfortable with, as I think that really helps. You can put together an odd couple and then if they win you're a genius, but it doesn't often happen that way. It's far better to go with the obvious strong partnerships.

'I was paired with Eamonn Darcy in the foursomes and the four-ball matches. I get on all right with Eamonn but from the personality standpoint there's absolutely nothing in common. If I'd been choosing the team I would have put together the personalities that blend. I would never have split the established team of Brian Barnes and Bernard Gallacher on the second day as Huggett did, and I suppose I would have chosen to play with Tommy Horton, Peter Oosterhuis or Howard Clark. You play your best golf when you're most comfortable.

'I played reasonably well the first day when Eamonn and I halved with Ed Sneed and Don January. When we lost the following day by 5 and 3 to Dave Stockton and Dave Hill, I played badly–and I certainly don't want to make Eamonn a scapegoat in any way for my bad play.

'After we had been beaten in the four-ball, we went straight off the course and had a bite to eat in the clubhouse. Then, as it was cold, we put on our rain gear and went back out on the course, walking to the 17th hole where we watched Mark James and Ken Brown. We were standing where their drives finished from off the tee. Apart from Nicklaus, the American team was out there pulling for their side, and of course there were thousands of British pulling for us.

144

Above left: *A golf-bag made for two. Tony and caddie Scotty Gilmour wait to tee-off at Wentworth, 1974.* Above right: *The end of an epic Ryder Cup match. Tony and Jack Nicklaus congratulate each other on the final green at Royal Birkdale, 1969.* Below left: *Vivien Jacklin.* Below right: *Tony with the then Prime Minister Edward Heath during the 1973 Ryder Cup match at Muirfield.*

'I was standing with Darcy, and Gallacher and Horton were behind us, when Brian Huggett came driving up in a cart and said to me, 'Where have you been–practising?'' I said, no, we've been having lunch. It was four in the afternoon and we hadn't eaten since breakfast.

'There were about 70 people standing round and Huggett went into a mad routine, shouting; ''You should have been out here supporting these lads.'' I replied: What the hell do you think we're doing here now? We've walked out from the clubhouse and we certainly can't play for these guys.

'So far as I was concerned Huggett was totally and utterly out of line. I went and took him to the other side of the fairway and told him that he was captain until the next evening, and this wasn't Crystal Palace football team–it was 12 different individuals. If he'd taken me aside it would have been different, but you can't say what he did in front of all those people.

'I got back to my room and about half an hour later Huggett 'phoned me to say he was sorry I had been dropped from the team the next day. I said that was all right, there was no need to apologise and put down the telephone.

'It was a personal thing and that's all. I play golf with him, I'm pleasant to the guy, we still say hello and get on.

'I think it's all a bit sad. A lot of other people knew what was going on but hardly anyone had the guts to say anything. Tommy Horton wrote a letter to Huggett, saying, I know you did what you thought was right–hoping Huggett would know that no one else did–but he still wrote a nice letter. Later, Oosty said something and I thought it was great, but Oosty's a straight shooter. Eric Brown to his credit came and asked me what I thought about being left out and I said I couldn't say anything about that–I was not arguing about being left out.

'I was embarrassed by the whole week, by the speeches saying we're going to win the Cup and keep it here . . . it's all rather stupid. It would be better to be honest. We know we've lost all these Ryder Cups in the past. We could say we would really like to give the Americans a good game, let the best team win, hope they enjoy the week and it's a pleasure to see them all, because nine times out of ten we're going home with our tails between our legs and why make it harder by living a lie–there's no point.

'The whole thing left a nasty taste in my mouth, but quite frankly I don't like team golf because I don't think golf is a team game. There's too much selfishness–you have to be your own man and do your own thing.

'I think it was a great concession on the part of the Americans to keep the Ryder Cup going under the new format. I thought there was a danger of it being scrapped altogether.

'I hope, now the European players are involved, that the matches will be closer and who knows, perhaps with a few victories, I'll get to like team games!

'I know a great many of the British players were against a change because it was instigated by Samuel Ryder as a contest between the two countries, but it has become almost totally one-sided.

'I'm sure the Europeans will make it closer and if that happens, then the Ryder Cup will be more enjoyable for everyone concerned.'

Tony does not criticise Huggett's action, but when it comes to dropping him from the team on that last day at Lytham, it is a pretty hard decision to justify, however badly he may have played. Take into account his past playing record and the fact that he had made the team every time since 1967. Remember also that early in 1977 he came second in the Bing Crosby tournament, a feat which certainly was not equalled by any other British golfer. He played American and British Tour events that year, and finished joint third in the Uniroyal International, and was only twice out of the top 17 during the whole British season.

The point is, would you prefer to have Tony Jacklin playing for you, than, for instance, a newcomer to the Ryder Cup team such as 20-year-old Ken Brown, who had never won an event in his life? Brown's best performance at that time had been joint second in the Greater Manchester Open. Or how about 23-year-old Mark James, whose claim to fame at that point was the 1976 Rookie of the Year and the Lusaka Open title in Zambia? Whom would you prefer to represent you against the Americans? Add to this, the fact that during the two days of foursomes and four-ball matches only Peter Oosterhuis and Nick Faldo, playing together, had wins to their credit. The only other bonus for the British team was the half gained on the first day by Tony Jacklin and Eamonn Darcy. All the other matches had been lost.

Later, when I saw Peter Oosterhuis in America, I asked him what he thought of the decision about Tony: 'I thought it was absolutely ludicrous dropping Tony from the Ryder Cup team on the last day,' said Peter. 'He won the Open over that course. Whatever happened, however he was playing, it was the captain's duty to have Tony play. Maybe he was playing poorly, but he is certainly not the 11th or 12th player in our team on any day.'

17: Past, Present and Future

TONY AND VIVIEN live comfortably in a seven-bedroomed house in Jersey with their three lively children, Bradley, Warren and Tina. The house is lived in and homely. It is efficiently run by Vivien, and although there is evidence of relaxation, there is also an air of hyperactivity.

The children all have a degree of restlessness and sensitivity about them. Tony jumps around and needs to be occupied when he is there, or is making plans to travel elsewhere. Vivien tries to present a picture of calm, but inwardly churns over and reacts inevitably to a life that is not always easy to hold together as a mother and wife.

There is an evident family bond. Tony and Vivien, who have been greatly dependent on each other through the years, have built up a strong and loving relationship.

In the kitchen Vivien proudly points out a poem that is hanging on the wall. Tony wrote it.

> I'm never happy when I'm not with you
> When I'm away I'm always blue
> Words can't say how much I care
> It's everything when I know you're there
> Stay by me all of my life
> My friend, my lover, my woman, my wife
> > with love, Tony

Tony is a sentimentalist. He's emotional, hyperactive, boyish, strong-willed. He's highly intelligent, and although his intelligence may have been channelled into one area – golf – his enquiring mind has made him delve deeper. He is charming to the point of getting away with whatever he wants. He's self-centred, intolerant, and dominant – obvious traits for any champion.

He is disarmingly honest: 'I'm a pain in the arse sometimes. I get so much pleasure out of things that everyone else has got to like what I like, and I find it difficult if they don't. I realise everyone can like and dislike what they want, but I'm irritated by people who don't know how to make the best of themselves.

'Success has meant that we're able to live our life the way we want to, which sounds totally selfish – and it is. But every individual I've met who has amounted to anything is selfish. People become afraid to admit it, because it sounds so wrong, so ungiving and thoughtless.

'My life is very organised when I'm playing golf. You can't be slapdash

Tony's happiest Ryder Cup, Royal Birkdale, 1969.

Friends and partners: Peter Oosterhuis and Tony at Muirfield during the 1973 Ryder Cup.

Tony in action during the Ryder Cup at Muirfield, 1973.

Vivien, Bradley, Warren and Tina with Tony at their Jersey home, 1979.

if you're flying round the world, on the road with a job to do. Most of the good players are organised. I do what I'm supposed to do for so much of the time that when I'm home I like doing things on the spur of the moment. I hate to be committed to the extent that if Viv says to me in the morning, what do you want for dinner I say, how do I know? I'm full, ask me when I'm hungry.

'I'm a perfectionist–I'm never satisfied. Maybe I have moaned sometimes on the golf course, but it's when I don't get the best out of myself and I get frustrated at hitting stupid shots that annoy me beyond belief.

'I believe in things being done right, and I don't think enough people care–they are sloppy. The main objective of living one's life is having pride in doing one's job, not just flashing a club at a ball a few times on the golf course and making money. That's not the object at all. You're doing something worthwhile to the best of your ability, and then having something worthwhile at the end. It's not like it's a breeze.

'There's not a minute of the day goes by when I don't think in some way about golf. I re-tiled my whole kitchen and as I was putting up the tiles I was thinking about golf. I clean the car and think about golf.

'Being lazy is just not caring about the thing. I believe with a passion that golf tournaments are not won on the practice tee, that it's nothing to do with hitting hundreds of balls. But I'm feeling pretty confident again, and I just might get myself back to a level of very high competitiveness.'

One factor that Tony has been missing over the last few years, is the ability to get 'up' at a tournament, to care enough to let it hurt to win.

The biggest blow in his entire golf career was not winning the Open Championship in 1972 at Muirfield when Lee Trevino chipped into the 71st hole. Tony doubts that he ever recovered and when he re-tells the story, he becomes so low and devastated by it, that the pain is almost too much to bear.

If one can pinpoint a moment in his life when things began to change, when it seemed no longer possible to sustain the enormous effort of the previous years, then Muirfield must be the focal point of it all. His life became something of a turmoil in the years that followed. Events overtook him and he lost his purpose.

Vivien comments: 'You get up so high and then you're right down. I was pleased when Tony won the two Opens, but although he had won them, I never expected him to go and win everything, even though I knew he was capable of being a great player. I hoped he'd do it again, and he was playing so well that I thought he might win in 1970 at St Andrews, in 1971 at Royal Birkdale, and in 1972 at Muirfield, which ended as an awful shock to his system.

'He was very young when he won. In those days people said you didn't mature until you were 30. I wish people hadn't made such a big thing of it. They said, what a pity you've done it so young, there's going to be a lot of pressure on you.

'There's a lot of pressure whenever you do it–there's no less at 35 than at 25. When you're at the top there is one level of pressure and you've got to take it. Tony did it, took it, and it was hard on him. But no one can take it away from him.

'The rushing round kills you, wears you out and slows you down but it makes money and we're not in it for laughs, it's a profession lasting only a short period of time. There's really no choice–you've got to work to make money, and who knows if they would last longer in playing terms without all the running around. It's difficult to pace yourself. Tony has tried for years and it has never really worked.

'He thinks he can handle everything, but he can't make up his mind and doesn't know how to go about doing everything. He's always into something, it might be clubs, or clothing, or something else, and all these things create problems.

'There was one stage when we never sat down for a meal at one time, because the 'phone was always ringing. I know it's part of it, there's nothing you can do about it and we had to go through it.

'We have only had one holiday in 12 years without golf clubs, and it would be nice to just have a family holiday but it never seems to happen. It's hard to get away from golf or from people who know golf and say, oh there's Tony Jacklin.

'At one point Bradley didn't want me to leave him and go away with Tony, but he accepted the fact when I told him that it was Tony's job and I would go with him to keep him happy.

'When Tina was little, she wouldn't accept Tony–she wouldn't speak to him. When he came in after being away, it was as though he wasn't there. Tony got quite upset about it, "she doesn't even notice me" he would say. I said, she's not prepared to accept your coming into her life and leaving it. She's not like the boys. She's a girl and I hope she is always like that, so that no one is going to walk over her, pick her up, come and go as they like. By the time she was about two, she accepted it. Now at four, she is perfect and she loves her Daddy.

'We enjoy life. I don't think anything has been that hard or that I've sacrificed anything in my life. We have a nice home, we don't have rows and the kids are healthy and happy.'

For Tony, his priorities lie in the same area: 'I've had success to a certain degree in golf, but I've succeeded with my family far more than with my golf. We're lucky the kids are healthy, intelligent, so much fun, and they say all the right things.

'I've never thought, Oh Christ, I've got to go home, but I've thought that about playing golf. Golf, after all, is just a game. Living a life is a game as well, but a hell of a lot more serious than hitting a white ball about. You're dealing with people, you've brought children into the world and they take first place–the next thing is golf.

'Golf is still important to me from the viewpoint of wanting to win, but

I will not give up my family life to achieve it – that's not what I want. One's outlook changes through experience and maybe other people would say, what a bloody idiot, only achievements matter but I happen to have my values in a different area.

'Some people live and die without seeing the light – they never know what the hell it's about. They live from day to day, work, and are miserable at it. They compare their life with that of everyone else. They are insecure and unhappy and they are not content enough to sit back and think, what is it really all about? What is our purpose?

'It's very difficult to answer, but I think it's to be a good human being, committing yourself to something and sticking to it, being a good egg. No, it's not that either. It's more than that. It's so many things. It's a wealth of experiences put together, forming an opinion, an idea, and going through with it as you feel it must be done, not shying away from it.

'I've got to live with me all my life and I'd hate not to like me inside. I'm not a puritan and I know I'm very good at forgetting things, or turning them round to make myself believe they were the right thing to do.

'Being happy means being comfortable with your existence, feeling that you are fulfilling yourself. Life is to be enjoyed. I'm seeing a lot, I've had a terrific education, I'm enjoying it, I'm happy with the people I know and the situation I'm in. I wouldn't change places with a single human being. I've got a job where I'll exhaust myself before I ever get it right. There's always a challenge and I need that.

'Success is partly being a father and running a home. You get guys who make £10 million and have nothing else. I'll die and I won't have changed much – but for me, it's a matter of what you do for you and yours.

'I find young people absolutely fascinating, marvellous. I would rather spend my time among children for the benefit of what they're going to say in the purest sense, and for the questions they'll ask – than be with opinionated adults. Children have a pure innocence, but as we grow older we inhibit ourselves.

'Children should be encouraged to think freely, do and say what they feel – it's bad for them to be suppressed. Bradley is a live-wire with a mind like a computer and it's very difficult for him to wind down. If he's not ready for bed at 8 pm he asks me if he can stay up and I say, sure, because I know how he feels. There's no point laying awake in bed thinking about it all. I'm probably not as strict as I should be about his bed-time.

'The greatest single thing to teach a child is a set of values. It's not easy, but it helps if you can let them travel and see different people and other ways of life. I want my children to be good, honest people, more than anything. Whether or not they are successful is immaterial to me.

'It may not be easy to be Tony Jacklin's son, but what about being Queen Elizabeth's son? It's up to me to make them realise that their life is their doing and they don't have to be champions of the world. What I did is nothing more than bar-room chat.

'I wouldn't mind if the kids wanted to play golf. I'd be the last one to push them into it, but it's a marvellous way of making a living, whether as a player or as a club professional. You meet a cross-section of people, you're out in the open, it's a great way of life.

'I want them to have a good education, but I don't know that I want them to go to public school and talk with a posh accent if in their heart of hearts they want to be on a golf course. It's far better to take them round with me.

'You've got to face problems with children as they arise. More than anything you must show them love and affection, and talk to them.'

For Tony, 1978 was a year of gradual repair from the frustration and turmoil of the previous years. He began to emerge from his depression, to come out of his shell, not to mind contact with people, which had been so difficult when he was really low.

'I feel happy,' said Tony, 'I'm enjoying my golf now, and I haven't been able to say that for ages.'

By June, in the Belgian Open, he was just one stroke behind the leaders after three rounds, but with a final round of 75 he finished in third place: 'It was a whole different feeling again. You get out of the habit and it was fun being involved among the leaders for a change. You have to use parts of your mind that you haven't used for a long time. Just playing tournament golf you don't use your upper consciousness because your concentration is not deep enough. When you're not under pressure, a part of you lies dormant.

'I felt good about being there and I found out that for the last few years I had let my mind wander. I had lacked concentration on the golf course. In my heart I know I'm good enough to win, but if your mind wanders it's useless. I have taken so much out of myself in the last few years – you're not burning it off the top when you're low, you burn it inside. Maybe I need to finish high a few times before I win again.'

In July, Tony missed the cut by one shot in the Open Championship at St Andrews for the first time ever. 'It was very disappointing but playing so badly the best I could have expected was to finish in the first 20 places. I'm a realist and I know that. I wouldn't tell anyone because I'm an optimist as well.'

In the German Open he won a silver grey Mercedes sports car with a hole-in-one.

Gradually, Tony retrieved his confidence in his golf as the year went on: 'I have progressed this year, so that I go to the first tee full of enthusiasm instead of wondering if I'll ever play well again. Honest to God, I feel I can go into any tournament now with a real chance of doing something and making it happen.'

Just how much Tony wants to happen is still a mystery. How far he will extend himself, only he can know. When he started out the first time, it was all quite uncomplicated.

'Before I became famous, I practised my signature – how the hell would it look right? I knew as sure as the sun was going to rise that I would be famous – it was so simple.

'When you're younger, you are motivated more easily. People say it must be easier the second time, but that is not so. When you've done it, you've done it, and subconsciously you think you haven't got to do it again.

'You're hungry on the way up and it's instinct. It's like the film *Star Wars* where you put the mask over your face, it's fight that thing, let go, let the force be with you. It's pure.

'It's when the dream becomes reality that things complicate it. You get waylaid, sway off course, money comes into it, and public opinion.

'Maybe you achieve your dream. Maybe with winning the two Opens my dream was fulfilled. Maybe I didn't want to be a great golfer over 30 years. It all depends what you want – you can be what you want to be.

'It's a dream that does it – a marvellous imagination, and you believe in it with a passion, so that everything else is superfluous. I know, because it happened to me.

'If there was one thing I could wish – and it may not be realistic – it would be that I had not wasted so much energy. I've got so much and often I've thrown it away going to places for the wrong reasons. I've done things, not because I wanted to, but because I thought I should do them. How do you get smart enough to use all your time properly?

'I could stand the pressure of winning and enjoy winning again. It's fun and something I know I can handle. If I don't do well it kills me, and I'm never getting the fruits of my labours.

'I've always had this thought about Frank Sinatra. Sinatra had two careers. He was way up, and then he was down. Then he went way up again.

'There must be a hell of a lot of satisfaction in that somewhere. I never thought in terms of it happening to me, but I think I'm capable of doing that.

'I wouldn't bet against my winning another Open if I get the bit between my teeth. When I get it rolling, I still feel exactly the same as I did in 1969.'

Index

Acknowledgments

Black and white
Associated Press, London 56 top right; Peter Dazeley, London 44 top left, 60, 74 top; Jacklin Collection title page, endpapers, 15 centre, 39 right, 44 bottom left, 65 right, 74 centre, 74 bottom, 129 left, 134 centre, 145 bottom left; Jacklin Collection–Associated Press 65 left; Jacklin Collection–Central Press 134 bottom, 145 top left; Jacklin Collection–Keystone Press Agency 56 top left; Mrs Doris Jacklin 15 top left, 15 top right, 15 bottom right; H.W. Neale, London 145 bottom right; Popperfoto, London 31 bottom left, 129 right, 134 top; Press Association, London 31 top right, 145 top right; Sports & General, London 31 top left, 31 bottom right; United Press International (UK) Ltd, London 39 left.

Colour
All-Sport, Morden–Don Morley 54, 71, 151; All-Sport–Steve Powell 123; Colorsport, London 25, 26; Peter Dazeley, London 152; Jacklin Collection 28 top, 28 bottom; Sporting Pictures, London 105, 106, 150; Syndication International, London 53, 72, 124, 149.

The luncheon plan and the letter from the late Duke of Windsor are reproduced by permission of Tony Jacklin.

The author wishes to thank Chris Plumridge, Peter Grosvenor and Frank Keating for their help and encouragement.

'You can please
some of the people
some of the time
but you can't please
all of the people
all of the time.
How well I know'

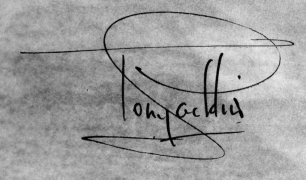